# The Dream Makers

DEREK WILSON

PROGRESS PUBLICATIONS

**The Author**

Derek Wilson is an established author with over 20 published works to his credit. He graduated from Cambridge in 1961 and has devoted himself full-time to writing since 1971. Most of his works to date have been on historical subjects and critics have commended his ability to 'incorporate original research into a popular format', 'take considerable pains to familiarise himself with recent scholarship,' and 'maintain a lively written style'.

ISBN 0 9508311 0 7

Printed in Great Britain for Progress Publications Ltd, Watercombe House, Wheddon Cross, Minehead, Somerset by Butler & Tanner Ltd, Frome and London

# Contents

# *Introduction*

On a Saturday in March 1982 ten thousand excited people thronged Britain's largest covered arena at Birmingham's National Exhibition Centre.

They were the Dream Makers.

They cheered and waved banners. They listened enthralled as speakers from America, Europe and all over Britain shared with them the secrets of success. They applauded the band of the Royal Marines, dancers and jazz players who had come to entertain them. They watched audio-visual presentations on a vast screen.

They were the Dream Makers.

They had come, as the convention slogan said, *Together Today for a Better Tomorrow*. For every one of the 10,000 people at that gathering, there were several others who would have loved to have been there to share the fun and excitement of Europe's biggest ever business meeting.

They, too, were the Dream Makers.

Every one of them is in the process of making his or her dreams come true—more money, a bigger house, a better car, freedom, setting the children up in business, travelling to see relatives in distant lands, supporting favourite charities. In short, they are making for themselves the lives *they* want instead of submitting to limitations imposed by background, education, lack of capital or low expectations.

Who are the Dream Makers?

They are ordinary folk who come from a complete cross-section of British society. And yet they are extraordinary in that they have associated themselves with the most original and exciting business concept of the last quarter century. They are part of an international organization linking over 1,000,000 happy, successful people and backed by a multi-million dollar international corporation.

Theirs is a success story which began in Britain in 1973, and unfolded during the years of inflation and recession that followed. That story continues and will become one of the best known and remarkable phenomena of the eighties and nineties.

It is the Amway story.

When I first came across Amway and began to learn something

of the way it was transforming people's lives I knew that here was a story that had to be told and that I wanted to tell it. So I set out on what was to become the most enjoyable journey that I have ever made round this country. I met hundreds of Dream Makers of every conceivable background and type—a plasterer's mate in Gloucester, a truck driver from Rugby, an evangelist in East Kilbride, a redundant Welsh steel worker, a blind businessman in Gosport, a widow living in the lovely Wye valley, a Yorkshire JP, an Essex factory worker, a teacher of Transcendental Meditation in Cornwall. It became a pilgrimage of sheer self-indulgence, for never before had I met so many cheerful, positive people, people who loved what they were doing, were proud of their success, and were happy to talk about it.

I owe a very real debt of gratitude to all the Amway distributors who talked with me so frankly. My wife, Ruth, did so much more than just transform my scrawl into something the printers could read. My sincere thanks to them all. I must also place on record my thanks to the General Manager and staff of Amway (UK) Ltd, who freely provided me with information and pictures and gave me access to Company records. In fairness to them and myself I must make it clear that this book is not financed by Amway (UK) Ltd nor does it pretend to present an 'approved' Company viewpoint. The opinions presented here are my own. This is Amway as I see it.

PART I

# A THING CALLED AMWAY

CHAPTER 1

# *The American Way*

'PRETTY smart, the two chaps who set all this going.'

'They certainly are,' I replied.

Then contrary currents of the laughing, chattering crowd swept us apart. I had time only for a brief glance at the man. Short back and sides. Sports jacket, old school tie. 'Military,' I thought. 'Very British. Establishment. Strange to hear him applauding a couple of Yanks.' But then the whole evening had been strange.

We were at an Amway rally in Bristol. The meeting was over. The bars were open. But seven hundred happy, excited people showed little intention of moving out of the conference hall. For two hours they had cheered and clapped as couples went on stage to receive 'recognitions': as an ex-plasterer's mate told how he had found the good life of wealth and luxury; as the General Manager demonstrated the Company's plans for a new warehouse and announced record-breaking business growth; as a young couple of keen Baptists explained how two years in Amway had given them greater freedom to devote to church work. The atmosphere had been electric. Now the audience jostled good-humouredly, as people greeted old friends, clustered around a display of Amway products or buttonholed speakers and company personnel.

To an outsider like myself it was all very bewildering. What was it that generated all this enthusiasm? What had this obviously diverse throng of people in common? The simple answer was 'selling soap'. Obviously, the simple answer had to be discarded. Whatever Amway was it was more than just a direct-selling organisation dealing in household products. My anonymous military friend was certainly right, the two chaps who had started Amway were certainly 'pretty smart'.

### *The co-founders*

Their names are Rich De Vos and Jay Van Andel. They do not like their story being called a rags-to-riches saga. True, they became millionaires before they reached middle age. True they started from very humble beginnings. But, they insist, that, as children, they were no worse off than others raised in the Depression years.

Their story, and Amway's story begins in Grand Rapids, an industrial city of a million and a half people thirty miles from the shore of Lake Michigan. Jay Van Andel was a quiet, serious lad, the son of a small garage owner who had emigrated from Amsterdam. De Vos, a couple of years younger, was more ebullient. He lived three blocks away from the Van Andels in his grandfather's home. His father was an electrician who always wanted to start his own business but never quite made it. What straitened circumstances really meant for most children in the years following the Wall Street Crash of 1929 was that they had to work for whatever they wanted. De Vos recalls vividly the methods he used to raise pocket money—working in petrol stations, doing a newspaper round, even selling left over vegetables door-to-door. Things were not quite so tough for Jay Van Andel. When he was sixteen his father gave him an old Model 'A' Ford.

It was that car that brought the two lads together. They had not really known each other before, although they were fellow students at Christian High School. Rich approached the older boy and offered to share petrol costs if Jay would drive him to school. That was the beginning of a lifelong friendship. The two lads found that they got on well together. They teamed up to go to ball games and movies, to ride out into the country, to fish in Grand River or camp by the lake shore. They did all the things that ordinary American boys did.

But those were not ordinary times. Cataclysmic events were rocking the old world to its foundations. Those events would swallow up the lives of millions of Rich and Jay's contemporaries. The survivors would find themselves in a new age, an age of changed relationships between nations, an age demanding different answers to old problems. The year that the two Michigan youngsters forged their friendship was 1940. Four thousand miles away, in the capital city of the world-spanning British Empire a newly-appointed leader was urging his people to prepare for 'their finest hour' as the stain of Nazi dictatorship spread across mainland Europe. Though Churchill might speak in public of the Commonwealth lasting a thousand years, he knew that the old order was changing. As he waited for Hitler's *Luftwaffe* to begin the siege of Britain, he turned towards F D Roosevelt, urging him to bring the USA into the conflict in defence of freedom and democracy. By degrees, Uncle Sam was persuaded to link arms with John Bull. A nation of 175,000,000 committed itself to the war effort and among those who enlisted for military service were two lads from Grand Rapids.

Van Andel and De Vos, like the majority of school friends,

could well have drifted apart during the war. They were separated for long periods, only meeting when service leaves coincided. They matured and developed as individuals, responding to new, different situations and personalities. Jay joined the US Army Air Corps as a private, decided he did not like being a dogsbody, worked hard for a commission and emerged at the end of the conflict as a first lieutenant. His friend, being younger, spent the early war years finishing his schooling. He was athletic and popular and was elected class president by his colleagues. Then, he, too, enlisted. Air Force service took him eventually across the Pacific to a base where he spent most of his time driving a truck. During these years Rich and Jay kept in touch. They wrote letters to each other, met whenever possible and, by the end of the war, they had decided that when they returned to civvy street they would set up in business together.

If you ask them why they made this commitment they will probably reply 'because we liked each other'. But there are deeper reasons for this lasting and extremely productive partnership. Although their personalities were very different they shared deeply held beliefs and convictions. They had absorbed the Calvinistic Christianity of their Reformed Church with its strong stress on individualism. War service had reinforced their ardent patriotism. Politically they were Republicans. They were convinced that the salvation of men and nations lay in individual enterprise. For themselves they were determined to make their own way in the world and they just knew that together they could achieve great things.

It should also be said that the time was right for them. They were about to prove the old truth that no power on earth can resist an idea whose time has come. After 1945 Americans regarded themselves, and were regarded by millions throughout Europe and Asia, as the champions of the free world. A fresh wave of immigrants poured into the United States from countries where the aftermath of war—ruined cities, homeless families, unemployed ex-servicemen, food rationing, street shelters, and broken lives—seemed to linger interminably. From the grey world of austerity Europe, men and women looked enviously towards the affluent, bright land of promise in the west, a land where anyone who believed in himself and was prepared to work could improve his lot. To the citizens of that land, much of whose wealth was being poured into funds for the recovery of late foes and allies, the envy seemed fully justified. The United States was about to fulfil her destiny. Political and economic influence on an international scale were hers. She had a mission as the world champion of democracy. She had the funds and could buy the expertise to spearhead scientific advance. Nothing on earth, it seemed, was impossible to her—and beyond earth the whole of space was waiting to be conquered. The self-confidence and ebullience of the nation was reflected in many of her people. In none did it shine more brightly than in Rich De Vos and Jay Van Andel. Starting from virtually nothing, they began a business career that was to make them both millionaires before they reached middle age.

Their first venture was the Wolverine Air Service. It was a natural development for two ex-servicemen who enjoyed working with aeroplanes. With fourteen hundred dollars, most of it borrowed, they bought a Piper Cub and, in 1946, began a flying school and charter business at a tiny airstrip near Grand Rapids. If you know you are going to succeed every obstacle changes into a challenge. That was the way these two young enthusiasts approached their commercial début. When the airstrip was flooded by spring rain they fitted floats to their plane and operated from the nearby river. The promised office building did not materialise. Jay bought a henhouse from a neighbouring farmer, erected it on site, cleaned it up, and they had a business HQ. They realised part of their land was empty and unproductive so they put up a hamburger stand and cooked the food themselves. After two years they had built up a flourishing business. They sold out and took a handsome profit. Why? Well, it had been hard work and the two young batchelors reckoned they deserved a holiday. For a year they went in search of fun and adventure. They bought a schooner and sailed her to the Caribbean. It was something they had long wanted to do, so they did it. Nor did they regret it for one moment, not even when they were shipwrecked and had to be rescued from shark-infested waters by a passing freighter.

When they came home they were ready to look for another commercial opening and prepared to consider absolutely anything that came their way. Nutrilite Products came their way. It was a company producing food supplements. It was registered in California. It was a direct selling business. Instead of employing a sales force the company supplied goods to individual agents who worked on a commission basis. It did not look particularly exciting but it was simple enough and Van Andel and De Vos reckoned they could make some money out of it until something better turned up. Very soon, however, they became more enthusiastic. The Nutrilite products were good. They consisted of tablets made from vitamin-rich greenstuff which were added to a normal diet to give a more balanced food intake. There were enough health-conscious Americans around to create a good demand, so that it was not difficult to sell the $19.50 packs. Retailing was not the only way to make money; you could also recruit new distributors and build income by creating your own network of agents. Rich and Jay worked hard. Their dynamism and enthusiasm were infectious and they steadily built up a large Nutrilite distributorship.

Successful as the Nutrilite system was the two young men could not be contained by it. Walt Disney's celebrated formula for success was 'dream, diversify and never miss an angle'. Whether or not Van Andel and De Vos had ever heard that dictum, it certainly summed up their own approach to business. They could see that the sales and marketing plan they were operating had potential far beyond the narrow world of food supplement pills.

Ten years passed in this way. During those years Jay and Rich both married. They sold their profitable businesses and concentrated on building one of the largest Nutrilite distributorships. They were so successful that, in 1959, Van Andel was offered the job of President of Nutrilite Products Inc. He turned it down, together with the five figure salary that went with it, because he could not break his partnership with De Vos.

That was one of many decisions made during the year of 1958–9, a year which proved to be crucial in the De Vos–Van Andel story. Problems at the Nutrilite headquarters in California were beginning to affect the organisation nationwide. It became obvious to the Michigan businessmen that their livelihoods were threatened by these difficulties. That concerned them, but not as much as the possible fate of the hundreds of distributors they now had within their organisation, many of whom had given up their jobs to go full-time into Nutrilite. The time had come to try to save the years of effort all of them devoted to building their individual distributorships. Taking a gamble, backing a hunch was nothing new to Van Andel and De Vos. But this time there was a difference; they were asking lots of other people to take the gamble with them. In the summer of 1958 they called their leading distributors to a meeting at Charlevoix and shared their ideas with them. No longer, they said, could they rely solely on Nutrilite products. They intended to look for other items to extend the range. Such was the confidence the two leaders inspired that, from the beginning they received almost unanimous backing from their distributors. With that encouragement, they took one more step in the early part of 1959, they formed the Amway Sales Corporation, a privately owned company, for the purpose of manufacturing and obtaining marketing rights in consumer products. After several more months of planning,

Amway, with its two distinct parts—a manufacturing company and a distributor organisation—was born.

### *How Amway works*

At this point in the story we have to pause in order to define exactly what Amway is. Well, it's rather like strawberry blancmange—easy enough to describe but impossible to convey the flavour. To appreciate just what makes this organisation tick you have to go and meet Amway people. That is why the greater part of this book is based on interviews I have had with distributors and Company employees. But we can go no further without some kind of definition.

Amway is a direct selling operation. The Corporation manufactures an ever-widening range of household products—soaps, polishes, cosmetics, cleaning agents, etc.—and these are retailed through the distributor organisation, which is made up of wholly independent people who use the products themselves and earn income by selling the goods and by building the organisation. That definition could be applied to many door-to-door outfits, but Amway is certainly not a door-to-door outfit. From very early on a distinct Amway philosophy developed. Distributors started to say and believe that Amway was more a people business than a product business. The whole operation was seen as a vehicle by which individuals could develop the American Way. And the American Way can be defined as success based on free enterprise and the family. Most distributors worked as husband and wife teams and they operated from their own homes.

If you have a marketing organisation you must have something to market. What? De Vos has gone on record as saying 'We decided to sell soap because people buy soap'. From the word go Amway relied on a line of products that people use on a regular basis. But there were already some very big manufacturers in this field. How could a company operating out of a basement (which is all Amway was in 1959) compete with giants like Unilever? The answer was to offer the customer better quality and greater economy. De Vos and Van Andel looked around for outstanding manufactures. A hundred and fifty miles away, at Trenton, on the outskirts of Detroit, was a small factory producing a remarkable liquid all-purpose cleaner called *Frisk*. The Corporation acquired trading rights and *Frisk* became their first marketable commodity. It proved highly successful and its successor, known more prosaically, as Liquid Organic Cleaner (L.O.C. for short) still tops the Amway popularity charts. As soon as the Corporation went into factory production, they set up research and quality control laboratories to ensure the highest possible standards of everything going out under the Amway label. Distributors and customers came to know that that label signified good, honest products which did not rely for their appeal on gaudy packaging, artificial bulking out or 'special offers'. Because the Corporation supplied direct to distributors they avoided the expense of middlemen, additional warehousing, advertising and a professional sales force. This meant that they could keep prices competitive. Many products (like L.O.C.) were marketed as concentrates which meant that the consumer was not paying for large quantities of water to be shipped around the country. In order to show their faith in their goods the Corporation established a full money back guarantee available to distributors and customers alike. Thus no-one starting an Amway distributorship ever had to fear financial loss. Rich and Jay figured that with good, economical, guaranteed products in everyday demand anyone could build an Amway business.

The statistics seem to prove them right. From turnover figures of half a million dollars in their first year of business, the Corporation expanded continuously. By the beginning of the 1980s sales had passed the billion dollar mark. This makes Amway one of the most staggering commercial success stories of the second half of the twentieth century. In its own field Amway's growth is spectacular and unique. Avon is the only direct selling organisation which is larger (around $3 billion at the beginning of the 1980s). Yet Avon has been in existence for almost a century. On these statistics there seems little reason to doubt the Corporation's assertion that it is poised to become far and away the world's largest direct marketing concern.

This is a record any commercial organisation would be proud of, especially in a period which has been dominated by economic recession and contracting markets. A conventional company could achieve it only by creative leadership, dynamic management at every level and a highly trained sales force. The astonishing fact about Amway is that its success depends on an organisation which has virtually no organisation. The thousands upon thousands of independent distributors who handle Amway products are linked by the most fragile of formal ties. They work not for wages, not from fear of or respect for the boss, but because they believe in Amway and because Amway pays well. So, it has to be said again that understanding Amway means understanding the ordinary people who are a part of it.

### *A good beginning*

But for the moment we must leave that and take up our story where we left it, in 1959. Those who joined Rich and Jay at the

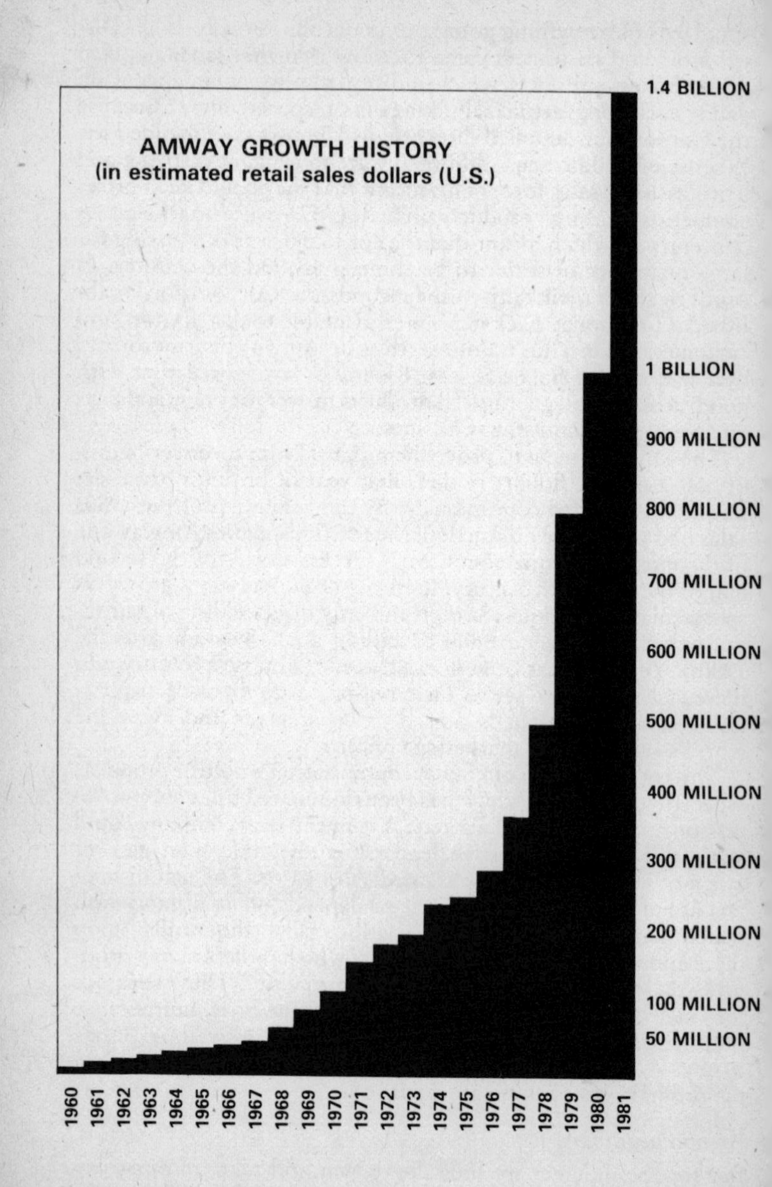
AMWAY GROWTH HISTORY
(in estimated retail sales dollars (U.S.)
1.4 BILLION
1 BILLION
900 MILLION
800 MILLION
700 MILLION
600 MILLION
500 MILLION
400 MILLION
300 MILLION
200 MILLION
100 MILLION
50 MILLION
1960
1961
1962
1963
1964
1965
1966
1967
1968
1969
1970
1971
1972
1973
1974
1975
1976
1977
1978
1979
1980
1981

beginning could not foresee the success that lay ahead. They had to have faith and determination and wait for results. In the event, they did not have to wait long. Within months they could see a staggering growth in the business. It was physically expressed in the rapid expansion of the Corporation's premises. Operations began in the basements of the Van Andel and De Vos homes. The friends had built themselves houses on land at Ada overlooking the Thornapple River. Lights were on in those houses well into the small hours almost every night as Rich and Jay and their wives packed orders, addressed envelopes, printed and stapled training manuals and turned their hands to any task that had to be done. When they were not at home the co-founders were often out taking meetings to show the Amway plan to prospective distributors. After a year they bought their first separate premises, an old filling station. Immediately a builder was contracted to erect a 5,600 square foot factory building. He had scarcely finished that, in 1961, when he was asked to start work on a 4,000 square foot extension. He has not left the site since. 1962 saw six new office buildings and warehouses appear. By 1963 more space was needed for the Corporation's fleet of trucks. The following year a new 20,000 square foot administrative building was one of the fresh projects on hand. Eventually Amway had bought three hundred acres of land around the existing complex on the banks of the Grand River. By 1980 the Corporation's headquarters comprised over a million square feet of well-planned industrial and administrative plant—and it was still growing.

*Some pioneer distributors*

All that growth is due to an increasing army of distributors. The influence of the co-founders is immense. They strike from the people they mix with. They are dynamic, enthusiastic and hard-working. When one of them walks into a room conversation dwindles and heads turn. They are widely respected as leading citizens and businessmen—Van Andel was, in 1979, Chairman of the US Chamber of Commerce; De Vos was strongly urged to accept the Republican presidential nomination in 1978. Throughout the entire world of Amway loyalty to the President (De Vos) and Chairman (Van Andel) is intense. Most of the million or so distributors have never met the co-founders yet the respect felt for De Vos and Van Andel and the system they established means that control can be limited to insistence on the simple code of ethics to which distributors pledge themselves. It is, therefore, rather remarkable that the business still works as it was designed to work in 1959. More than two decades have passed. Amway has spread into many countries around the world. Yet the original concept has not changed and the methods used to put the concept into effect are virtually the same as they were over two decades ago.

In that time some very striking men and women have joined the distributor organisation. They have made an enormous impact on the lives of thousands. Some have been highly successful. They have exercised an influence within the world of Amway, bringing their own emphases and styles to bear upon the business.

### *The dynamic duo of Dallas*

Say 'Dallas' to most Englishmen and they will think of 'J.R.' and the other fictional members of the Ewing family whose loves and hates held millions of TV viewers spellbound over several weekly episodes of their glamorous saga. Of course, real people live in this Texan oil city and some of them lead lives scarcely less glamorous than the Ewings. They are not all oil millionaires. At least one couple are Amway millionaires. Dan and Bunny Williams have reached the highest level in the organisation (Crown Ambassador). They have thousands upon thousands of distributors in their line of sponsorship, which encircles the globe. They have an income which amply sustains their expensive cars, their fabulous, luxury apartment in one of Dallas's most exclusive blocks and their frequent trips around the States and overseas.* They have more friends than they can count—genuine friends who love them for the help and encouragement they have given, not sycophants like those who suck up to the mythical J.R., solely because of his wealth. No-one begrudges the Williamses their money, for they have earned it and they have come to it after years of struggle. Dan always wanted to make a career in the Navy but that was cut short by a nervous complaint he just could not overcome; he stuttered. He tried every kind of treatment. Nothing worked. The affliction also hampered his progress in civvy street. By 1966 he was working for a giant chemical combine—and he was stuck. Promotion was slow, salary inadequate for the family's needs. Then Amway came into his life—and the stutter went out. It was as simple as that—cause and effect. The Amway plan really grabbed him. He loved talking to people about it. He enthused, and as he enthused his self-consciousness vanished. For the first time in his life he did not care whether people laughed at his stutter or not. He had something good to tell them and nothing was going to stop him.

* Since this was written Dan and Bunny Williams have moved to a magnificent residence in California.

And the new growth of self-confidence smothered the stuttering weed.

*From the beat to Millionaire's Row*

Fort Lauderdale, like Dallas, is also a chunk of solid gold real estate. It lies on Florida's Atlantic coast just north of Miami. It is where some of America's wealthiest citizens go, to live all year round in sumptuous waterfront homes or to spend the winter in luxury condominiums. Among the most palatial residences overlooking the blue ocean is the one belonging to an ex-New York cop and his wife, Charlie and Elsie Marsh. Charlie's attitude is, 'my story proves that anybody can do it who wants it badly enough'. He emerged from a less-than-indifferent school career to face the workaday world with virtually no qualifications. After trying a number of other jobs, he settled down as a policeman in the mid 1950s. The Marshes lived a drab, inner-city existence and there was nothing to suggest that the future held anything better for them. It was a relative in another part of America who introduced them to Amway—but not by showing them the business; he simply sold them some shoe spray. It was only when Charlie phoned Ada about getting replacements that he began to realise there was more to Amway than selling products. HQ put him in touch with a local distributor. The Marshes had the business explained to them and joined. Limited as Charlie's education was, he immediately grasped one esssential fact: 'I was in something where I was the variable. There were no excuses.' He immediately began sponsoring people—or trying to. In the first few weeks he set up thirty-one meetings in his home. And for thirty-one evenings no-one turned up. Most people would have shrugged their shoulders and said 'It doesn't work'. Charlie gritted his teeth and said 'It does work, so I've got to take it really seriously'. He went to his colleagues—many of them the very people who had let him down before—and asked them again, this time with a new conviction and determination. And it worked. It worked so well that Charlie resigned from the force three months later, found that he and Elsie had a million-dollar group at the end of their first year, and that business rocketed to take them to the Crown level inside six years. The day the Marshes received their Crown Direct Distributor awards from Rich De Vos was a great day for them and for Amway because they were the first couple to attain what was then the top level. The Marshes reached the millionaire bracket by enthusiastic sponsoring and many Amway distributors regard them as trailblazers. They showed just how important it is to maintain a balance between retailing and sponsoring. Back in 1964 someone made a few cents profit by selling Charlie Marsh some shoe spray. If he had shown Charlie the full potential of the business instead ... There is a moral there and the Marshes have drawn it.

*Globetrotters*

Most successful business people guard their 'trade secrets' closely, and with good reason: if competitors get in on the act, profits dwindle. Not so in Amway. The top distributors are always in demand, to speak at meetings and share their experience and advice. That is why Dan Williams and Charlie Marsh were on the platform at a seminar in Dallas in 1970. Among the audience of eager-to-learn distributors was a young couple from Houston. Joe Logan was an electronics engineer at the Manned Space Centre and was heavily involved in the Apollo project. Mary was a secretary working on the same heavily guarded complex. Being a part of the world's most advanced space programme would strike some people as being exciting. In fact, the moments of drama were rare. For most employees, working at the Centre was routine—just another job in industry. In the few years since he had graduated from Auburn University, Alabama, Joe had become somewhat disillusioned with industry. He had discovered that pay and prospects had very little to do with how hard you worked. A man earned the rate his union negotiated whether or not his heart was in his job. So he was ready to try Amway when he and Mary were shown the plan by some old friends. As for Mary, well, she had come from England at the age of 18 looking for fortune and fulfilment in the 'land of promise', so she was happy to give Amway a try. The business went reasonably well, and even better after the Dallas seminar. Joe recalls how some of his workmates made fun of his 'soap business' and how he had the last laugh when he handed in his notice because Amway was already paying him many times more than the Space Centre.

From early days in the business Mary had the dream of sharing Amway with old friends and relatives in England. In 1973, when Amway (UK) Ltd was set up, she and Joe crossed the Atlantic and spent four happy years helping to establish the American Way in Britain. By 1977 they had an Emerald business (see p. 25) in America and another in the UK. The income flowing in on both sides of the ocean was sufficient for anything they might reasonably want. They took a seven months' round-the-world holiday and Joe speaks of the thrill of realising that they now had complete freedom and could settle anywhere they wanted. After a leisurely trip home on the *QE2* they decided that where they wanted to settle was in Walnut Creek, an exclusive residential area near San Francisco. There they now enjoy the very good life. Yet like so many Amway folk they talk most enthusiastically about non-material things. The Logans are very excited about international sponsoring and have contributed a great deal to the spread of the Amway idea across national boundaries. Joe recalls sitting on a beach in Majorca with Amway distributors from Britain and Germany thinking 'it wasn't all that long ago that our countries were engaged in a great conflict and here we are brought together by a pretty neat business idea'.

*Amway goes international*

The development of the Logans' British business was made possible by the Amway Corporation's international sponsoring arrangements. Van Andel and De Vos always knew that free enterprise was a universal concept and from the earliest days they planned for Amway's overseas expansion, but events overtook even Rich and Jay's optimism. The Canadian border is less than a hundred and fifty miles from Ada as the crow flies. There were very soon customers and distributors on the other side of that border and a subsidiary had to be set up to service them. Then came Quebec and, although the province was a part of Canada, it was still a different culture. When the business was established there, Amway, for the first time, had to produce literature and labels in a language other than English. It was not long before Spanish had to be added, for Amway expanded next into Puerto Rico, technically an American dependency but, again, a distinct culture. So far the growth pattern had been inevitable. Any move into distant lands had to be much more carefully planned. Above all, the Corporation and the distributor organisation had to work in harness. There was no question of employees from Ada sponsoring in a new territory, as well as organising product distribution. Sponsoring by distributors was the only way international growth could occur. Any distributor could sponsor in any country where Amway was represented or where Amway was about to start business.

The 1970s might be called the decade of Amway international. The first big jump was Australia. The operation began there in 1971. Thanks to careful preparation, the business got off to a sound start. The urge to open up Great Britain to Amway opportunity was now irresistible. Hundreds of American, Canadian and Australian distributors had contacts there. The prospect of starting a business in the 'old country' was very attractive. For the Corporation the UK had a double appeal: it was a potentially good market in itself and it would be a springboard into Europe.

So Amway came to Britain in 1973. The following year saw the opening of the Hong Kong office. In 1975 it was West Germany, 1976 Malaysia, 1977 Eire and France, 1978 the Netherlands, 1979 Japan. As the world turned into the 1980s Belgium and Switzerland joined the Amway family. With Amway actually *working* in thirteen different countries the original judgement that it is a universal concept seems to have been proved pretty conclusively.

The interesting thing is that it works in basically the same way everywhere. The stories of startling personal success which happened in the USA, happened again to distributors in other parts of the globe. Take, for example, Peter and Eva Muller-Meerkatz. Peter interested himself in Amway soon after it started in Germany, not because he wanted to join but because he needed material for his PhD thesis. He was a young research student working in the field of business theory and his particular line of study was the pyramid companies. As soon as he examined the Amway operation he realised that it was a unique business concept and certainly had nothing to do with pyramid selling. He also realised something far more important: this was a business that he and his wife should be in on. The couple worked with total conviction and enormous energy. They became West Germany's most successful distributors and they set a new record by reaching Crown level in a staggering thirty-three months.

### *Why does it work?*

There has to be an explanation for the phenomenal success Amway has notched up. Part of that explanation is the co-founders. They inspire an admiration of a type and intensity not usually accorded to businessmen. They lead by example and they genuinely care for the people in their organisation. They actually *want* their success to be shared by other people. In a book outlining his practical creed, De Vos describes some of the business ventures he and Van Andel started, and he draws this moral:

> 'What does all this say? Give things a chance to happen! Give success a chance to happen! It is impossible to win the race unless you venture to run, impossible to win the victory unless you dare to battle. No life is more tragic than that of the individual who nurses a dream, an ambition, always wishing and hoping, but never giving it a chance to happen ... Millions of people are that way about having a second income, or owning their own business, and Amway is designed somewhat in response to that need ... For the individual in that position there is only one thing left after all the arguments are weighed

and all the costs measured. Do it. Try it. Quit talking about it and do it.' *

What Van Andel and De Vos have done is set up an organisation within which anyone prepared to take up that challenge has a good chance of succeeding. It is a hard fact of life that most people fail; that is they never achieve what, in their heart of hearts, they would like to achieve. Since they do not like to admit failure, they console themselves by attributing their poor performance to external factors. Fate has dealt them a poor hand: they have had to their best against severe odds. If only things had been different they would have done better. If only they had had a better education. If only they had had some capital. If only they knew the right people. Quite simply, Amway takes away the 'if only'. It says 'Here's a business of your own. You don't need education, social position, special skills or enormous capital reserves. If you don't believe that ordinary people can succeed in this business, look around at the thousands of them who already have and whose life style has changed dramatically for the better'.

Many people I spoke to found it difficult to pinpoint exactly why they are part of the Amway operation. For them it just 'feels right'. They like the impeccable ethics of Amway. They like being part of something that

> 'brings together people from all walks of life, people with varying religious convictions, political affiliations, nationalities, languages, ethnic backgrounds and racial origins; people who come together as business associates in agreement on the principles of free enterprise, willing to work together and help one another achieve financial independence.' †

There are plenty of distributors who will admit that they joined for the money and the good things money brings—Cadillacs, houses on millionaires' row, freedom, Amway seminars in Hawaii, Acapulco, and Monte Carlo, Caribbean cruises on the Amway yacht *Enterprise*—but that their attitudes have changed. Now the aspects of the world of Amway they value most highly are new friends and the ability to help others realise their dreams. Perhaps Andrew Taylor, an Emerald Direct distributor from Hereford, put his finger on it 'I had my own business before and sometimes I had to do things that the better side of me didn't like. I always wanted to be good and in the commercial world that isn't always possible. But in Amway I can be the sort of person I want to be.'

* *Believe*, pp. 28–9.

† *Ibid.*, pp. 28–9. *Amway Annual Report*, 1977.

Although Amway is big and growing more rapidly than almost any commercial enterprise in the world, it seems to reflect many of the virtues of a cottage industry—good honest dealing on a person-to-person basis. And this is at a time when big business is coming under mounting criticism. In his book *Third Wave*, Alvin Toffler quotes a significant study produced for the Harvard Business School in 1977.

> 'the study revealed that about half of all consumers polled believe that they are getting worse treatment in the market-place than they were a decade earlier; three-fifths say that products have deteriorated; over half mistrust product guarantees.'

Toffler quoted a spokesman for a top US firm of accountants as saying 'public confidence in the American corporation is lower than at any time since the Great Depression'. Yet, in November 1979 when the *Saturday Evening Post* ran an article on Amway, the reporter noted 'a difference between Amway and so many of the industrial giants of the famous *Fortune* magazine top "500" list'. That difference he defined very simply as the fact that, for Amway, people came first. The Corporation has, from time to time been scrutinised by government bodies and consumer organisations, especially in the early 1970s when the pyramid selling scandal was at its height. On every occasion it has left the court without a stain on its character. For example, in 1979 the US Federal Trade Commission concluded a four-year investigation into certain Amway activities with the verdict that the Corporation had 'injected a vigorous new competitive presence into a highly concentrated market'.

*Can it continue?*

Amway has experienced almost a quarter of a century of fantastic growth. It has enabled thousands of people to realise their dreams. And all this has happened at a time when nations and business enterprises have been staggering from one economic crisis to another. Surely the bubble must burst sometime? All the Amway people—distributors and Company employees alike—say that it will not.

There is no doubt that the parent Corporation believes in the permanence of all it stands for

> 'It is a fundamental belief at Amway that the free enterprise philosophy will continue to thrive—even across and through cultural barriers—as more and more people are given the opportunity to share in the rewards of individual enterprise around the world'.*

* *Amway International Annual Report*, 1979.

In 1973 this philosophy was given tangible expression when the Centre of Free Enterprise was opened at Ada, a spectacular building and the focal point of the whole Amway complex. There, exhibitions are housed and courses run to instruct people in the values which undergird the De Vos–Van Andel empire. It is the headquarters of the Free Enterprise Institute, an educational foundation set up to spread the gospel of liberty and integrity in commerce. As long as the De Vos and Van Andel families are around there will be no watering down of that gospel, for they own Amway Corporation, lock, stock and barrel. There are no shareholders or boardroom cabals to enforce changes of policy. The holdings of this privately-owned corporation are impressive and all seem to be in keeping with the aims of Amway. As well as the billions of pounds' worth of industrial and administrative plant round the world, the fleets of lorries and vans, the railway rolling stock, the two BAC 1–11 jets and the fleet of Cessnas, Amway owns the Nutrilite company with its thousands of acres of plantations in California and Puerto Rico. They have bought an old hotel in Grand Rapids, restored its 1920s decor, renamed it the Amway Grand Plaza and made it a luxury hotel for conferences and accommodating guests. They own the Mutual Broadcasting System which relays news and advertising through affiliated stations all over the USA. They run the Amway Mutual Fund, an investment organisation managed by top professionals which gives distributors the opportunity to make still more money from their surplus Amway income while at the same time supporting the American free enterprise commercial structure. There is also an Amway Distributors' Association which brings many benefits, including medical insurance to members. Amway is expanding so rapidly and in so many directions that any attempt to describe it is doomed to almost instant obsolesence.

The same is true of the product range. At any one time hundreds of new lines are being considered. Some reach the testing stage. Only the few that comply with Amway's high standards go into production. The days when Amway was a 'soap-selling business' are long past. In the USA there are over 3,000 items in the product range—household products, electronic equipment, cosmetics, jewellery, clothes and a host of other commodities. The time is not far off when the Amway slogan *Shop Without Going Shopping* may be a complete reality for American households. The Corporation already has a flourishing catalogue business and within a few years will be able to supply virtually all everyday needs with the exceptions of perishable foodstuffs. What is true for the USA today will be true for

Amway's overseas markets tomorrow. The product range is gradually being increased in each area at a well-monitored rate. There seems little reason to doubt that Amway will become the largest marketing organisation in each country which it operates. This is one answer to the suggestion that the Corporation will eventually achieve market saturation, and so stop growing. When there is almost no limit to the range of goods there is almost no limit to the available market.

### *A foretaste of the twenty-first century?*

Ours is a radically changing society. The microchip, the computer, the contraceptive pill, the nuclear capability are among many developments revolutionising politics, industry, family life and traditional values. Our children's world will be vastly different from our own. In the future more people will work at home, linked by a battery of electronic devices which will make it unnecessary to concentrate large numbers of people in offices. The majority of employees will work shorter hours; the 'working week' will become an obsolete concept. Consequently people will be freer to organise their leisure time as they please. New patterns of commercial activity will develop as the existing market system collapses under its own weight:

> '... the growing complexity of distribution, the interpolation of more and more middlemen ... appears to be reaching a point of no return. The costs of exchange ... are now outrunning the costs of material production in many fields. At some point this process reaches a limit. Computers, meanwhile, and the emergence of a prosumer-activated technology [i.e. small commercial units, often the home, which both produce and consume goods] both point to ... simplified rather than more complex chains of distribution. ...' *

Simplified chains of distribution, people working from home, greater personal freedom—it all has a familiar ring about it. Perhaps Amway, so far from having a dubious future, is a foretaste of the future in the present.

Amway is the sort of unique operation that tempts the observer into such speculation. But it exists in the here and now and that is where it must be judged. In the last analysis the future of Amway is in Amway people. If they have and maintain their conviction, then it is difficult to see what can stop this rolling bandwaggon. Conviction is one quality I have seen in every

* A. Toffler, *The Third Wave*, p. 285

distributor and Company representative I have met. I remember talking with Sandra Taylor, a vivacious young businesswoman and one half of one of England's very successful Amway partnerships. I asked her if she ever woke up in a cold sweat from a nightmare in which she had seen the great Amway dream crumble into dust. The look of astonishment on her face was genuine. 'For a start,' she said 'I just know it couldn't happen. We have built up such a wonderful organisation of great people. So many of them are our personal friends.' I was not letting her off the hook as easily as that. 'But couldn't it be,' I suggested 'that the only thing binding these friends together is mutual self-advantage!' She shook her long brown hair. 'When you've seen people from every class and background come together on equal terms and really enjoy being together—Well that's friendship on a deep level. Amway people are great people and I want to spend the rest of my life being with them.'

When someone says that sort of thing to you, you realise you are dealing with an organisation which is very much more than just a successful business.*

* For further information on the foundation and growth of Amway Corporation see Charles Paul Conn, *The Possible Dream,* New York, 1977.

CHAPTER 2

# *But is it the British Way?*

KEN and Jane Roberts are a 'nice' couple. It is an overworked adjective but, in this case, it is the right one. Well-dressed—without being ostentatious—relaxed, and quiet; they are the kind of people you take to instinctively. They make you feel comfortable. They are both around forty and have two children of school age. Their tastefully-furnished house in a quiet cul-de-sac of a Welsh border town is an extension of their personality. For, while everything about it is elegant and tidy, a typewriter (operated by the Roberts' full-time secretary, who is also an Amway distributor) chatters constantly in the background, punctuated frequently by the telephone bell, and you soon realise that beneath the calm there is considerable activity. Ken and Jane were among the first recruits for Amway's UK enterprise and they have built their business to the Diamond level. They now lead and guide several thousand distributors and are extremely active—taking meetings, speaking at rallies, keeping in touch with their organization by phone and letter.

Of all the British pioneers I spoke to it was the Roberts who, I felt, communicated most clearly just what the early days of Amway in this country were like. Amway is people, people welded together into a voluntary organization. It has many of the characteristics of a church, society or club. It is not like a conventional business in which management controls the work force largely because it holds the purse strings. Amway only succeeds when thousands of individuals and couples decide, off their own bat, that they want it to succeed. That means that in Britain, as in any other country, Amway had to start from scratch, had to build up from small beginnings. The parent organization knew that it could not sweep in and 'show the British how to do it'. There could be no multi-million pound advertising campaign, no impressive launch with bands and banners and free scotch for the press. The work could only be done by British people. Distributors had to be recruited, distributors with sufficient strength of character to work 'in the cold'. They would have to develop their own methods with little back-up from their distant sponsors. They would have to commend an idea as yet unproved in this country. The only success stories they could tell would be about distributors in other lands. Yet somehow they had to convince friends and neighbours that 'it could work here'. I wanted to know how the Roberts had faced up to this challenge.

In 1974 Ken was a senior supervisor with Rank Xerox. The work was reasonably paid but even with Jane going out to a part-time job and Ken trying his hand at selling pots and pans in the evenings they had little money for luxuries. They did not own their own home and they were heavily in debt. Their social life was virtually non-existent, partly because there was little spare cash and partly because they were rather shy. When the Amway plan was shown to them they saw its potential and worked at it. And it really was work. Ken readily admits that success came slowly. Amway was something totally new on the British scene and two essential ingredients of success—belief and experience—could only be accumulated gradually. There would be no short cut. Even American distributors who came over to help set up a UK operation found that their own well-tried methods did not always work in a different environment. So what persuaded the Roberts to keep going? 'Faith,' said Ken emphatically. 'We had sheer faith that things would get under way.' Within a few weeks Jane gave up her job in order to concentrate on Amway. It took them sixteen months to reach Direct Distributor level and the thrill of receiving their pins from Jay Van Andel marked a real turning point for them. Exciting as that was, however, Jane has no doubt that another event moved them more profoundly. That was seeing their first distributors 'go Direct'. 'You don't know what its like helping someone else to make it, until it happens,' she said.

Ken had always been discontented with his position at Rank Xerox. He dreamed of being his own boss but knew that he would never have the capital to make that possible. Three years after starting his Amway business Ken Roberts was a free man. He and Jane had long since passed the point of having any doubt about Amway but they were still concerned about progress nationwide. Ken has obviously thought a great deal about those early years and this is his considered opinion of them: 'The greatest need was for personal development by the hard core of distributors. Attitudes throughout the country were not good in those years. It was a depressing time economically, and people found it difficult to believe in themselves. Inevitably, Amway folk were affected by the general climate. When that hard core of distributors had gone through a period of personal development, then we were able to start putting things together, to decide what we needed in the way of books, tapes and other aids.' From then on the growth rate increased dramatically. What has happened since about 1978 can only be described as an 'explosion', according to Ken. And, adds Jane, as more people succeed and reach the higher levels it becomes easier to interest prospective distributors. The growth curve can only get steeper.

Anyone looking at the Roberts might well find them a persuasive argument for climbing on the Amway bandwaggon. A new house, and car, freedom to plan their life and work as they please, frequent trips abroad—all these have come their way in seven years and they see no reason why their future plans should not be realised. These include a larger house, and all the modern equipment to go in it, private secondary education for the children and lots more travel. But when they look back at the difference Amway has made to them, Ken and Jane agree that it is not the material rewards that matter most. 'We have more friends than we can possibly count; friends all around this country, friends in other countries, and that is worth a lot. We have developed enormously as individuals. We are more self-confident. We appreciate things and people more. We're just happier.' There didn't seem to be any answer to that.

### *The beginnings*

The Roberts had given me one picture of Amway's beginnings in the UK I now needed others to compare and contrast with it. I wanted to get the full flavour of those far-from-easy days before the dramatic surge of success began. I knew that my story needed a good foundation and that this could only be provided by the pioneers. I also knew that the information would have to be collected quickly before people's memories became coloured by nostalgia or clouded by later success. First, however, I needed the basic facts and these were easily obtained from Company literature and personnel.

It was John Dodds, General Manager 1976–1981, and one of the first members of the company's staff, who explained an important principle to me. 'Once Amway goes into a country, it's there for good. It is a fundamental part of the Corporation's ethic that it will never abandon its distributors.' This made good sense both in terms of the obvious Christian motivation of the founders and also in terms of commercial stability. If Amway had a failure in a particular country and simply pulled out, leaving its distributors high and dry its avowed principles of helping individuals achieve their dreams would lack credibility and its chances of pioneering new markets would be much impaired. This being the case, Amway headquarters had to research the UK market carefully before making the large financial commitment necessary to establishing a transatlantic subsidiary.

Yet it was not simply a matter of commercial research. There is always a double impetus behind the establishment of an Amway operation in a new country; the initiative comes both from the Corporation and the distributor organisation. De Vos, Van Andel and their team looked very closely at Britain in the early seventies before deciding that the commercial and political climates were right for their style of free enterprise. As we have seen, the founders of Amway had always regarded overseas expansion as inevitable. The hardy plant of free enterprise, they reasoned, could take root in any soil not poisoned by oppressive tax laws or extreme socialism, and the strong contacts which have always existed between America and Britain suggested that the UK would be a very fertile ground. At the same time pressure was building from distributors in the USA and Canada (and, to a lesser extent, Australia). They had relatives and friends in the UK with whom they wanted to share their exciting business. Some of those relatives and friends had already heard of Amway through letters or on visits to the States. For them the American dream would have to remain a tantalising vision until they had a subsidiary company in their own land. The system of international sponsoring encouraged existing distributors to cross frontiers with the Amway idea.

By mid-1972, with their companies in Canada and Australia well established, De Vos and Van Andel were ready to take the plunge. A small warehouse and office unit was rented at the newly-established town of Milton Keynes. Staff were hired. Several executives were sent from Ada to set the UK operation on its feet and Amway (UK) Ltd was incorporated as a subsidiary company. In May 1973 the new office opened its doors for business. But who was it going to do business with?

The answer to that lay largely in the hands of two American couples, Joe and Mary Logan and Don and Angie Nellenbach. Mary and Angie had both gone from these islands as young women, seeking fortune and adventure in the USA. Both had married Americans. The Nellenbachs lived and worked in New York State, the Logans in Texas. Both couples started Amway businesses in the 1960s, both had reached Emerald level. By 1973 the girls were hankering for a sight of home—Mary for the green grass of England and Angie for the greener pastures of Ireland. The start of Amway (UK) Ltd, seemed to be the ideal opportunity for a transatlantic trip. The Logans and the Nellenbachs came over and settled down, both in Kenilworth, that same year. They worked the business as they knew it had to be worked: they took every effort to make contacts by speaking to neighbours and people at the shops, by joining tennis clubs, golf clubs and various societies, by frequenting the 'local'. They sold the seventeen products which, at that time, made up the Amway UK range. They held meetings and Mary recalls how often Joe muddled up pounds and dollars when explaining the marketing plan to English listeners. They sponsored new people into the business. They lived on the continuing income from their US businesses while they watched their British groups grow.

Mary told me just how tough those first months were. 'We went down to HQ at Milton Keynes at least once a week to talk Amway with *somebody*. 'Somebody' was the permanent British staff of just four people. Recruiting went slowly. It was difficult for people to realise that they were present at the birth of something very, very big. But the few people who did grasp the potential of Amway became close friends. Mary remembered Geoff Smith, a plasterer from Gloucester, who used to travel to Kenilworth with Jenny, his wife, and their little group of distributors. 'They would occupy one whole row at a rally. Then they'd all sleep on the floor over at our house and haul products back with them next day. We take our hats off to those who stayed with us through the "thin" times, when large price rises were normal, when deliveries were erratic and very slow, when the meetings were not very exciting and when the UK *Amagram* was one sheet of black and white mimeographed paper.' The Logans had reached the Emerald level in sixteen months in the USA. In Britain it took them four years.

But slowly the success came. The American pioneers and the first British distributors certainly experienced disappointment and depression but there was excitement, too. 'There is nothing more wonderful than to sponsor a new couple and see them fire.' That was what Joyce Greaves told me as she looked back, almost wistfully, to the early days.

*A Coventry success story*

To know Joyce and her husband, Al, is to love them. They are warm-hearted, down-to-earth Midlanders who will go anywhere and do anything to help someone in need. Wealth and success have not gone to their heads. They describe themselves as 'ordinary folk' and they get quite a kick out of the apparent contradiction between this image and their lifestyle. When I met them they were still chuckling over something that had happened recently. 'I met this businessman and mentioned to him that we had an opportunity that might interest him,' Al explained. 'Well, he looked at me and pooh-poohed the idea. I bumped into him again yesterday in town and said I'd just brought my car in for servicing. "Oh," he said, "what sort of car have you got?" I said, "That's it over there." (Al drives an immaculate white Mercedes.) Well, the poor bloke, his eyes nearly popped out of his head. "You bought that out of your business?" "That's right," I said. And do you know, he actually went down on his knees on the pavement. "Tell me more," he said, "Tell me more."'

The Greaves were among the first UK distributors and, unlike some others, they stuck with it through the difficult early years to reach their present very successful position. That was why I had come to see them. Ten years ago stocky Al Greaves spent most of his time behind the wheel, not of a smart car but of a long-distance lorry. At that time his effervescent wife worked as a punch card operator. They lived in a terrace house in Al's home town of Coventry with their two young sons and they thought there must be something more to life. 'We'd tried all sorts of things to make money on the side,' said Joyce. Al had explored the possibility of raising finance to buy his own truck but when he thought seriously about starting his own business, Al admitted ruefully, 'I knew the capital wasn't there and I knew I hadn't got much brains.' Joyce had taken on an agency for selling occasional tables, 'but they all warped and nobody wanted any more'. Therefore they were quite excited when friends in America wrote to them about a part-time business involving no capital outlay. They had to wait two years for their friends to come over and tell them about Amway.

It was then September 1973. Al was away on a trip but Joyce listened eagerly to the sales and marketing plan. She watched her friends covering a sheet of paper with figures and circles. They meant nothing. She listened to their excited description of the Amway operation and she could not see what they were so enthusiastic about. She made polite noises but when Al arrived home at two o'clock the next morning, eager to hear about an incredible business opportunity all his crestfallen wife could say was 'It's selling soap'. They both decided they wanted nothing to do with it but Joyce felt too embarrassed to tell her friends. Al said, 'Well, look, it only costs a couple of pounds. Join to please them. Then, when they've left for the States you can return your kit and get your money back.'

And that is exactly what Joyce would have done if she had not met the Logans. Joe and Mary tried to explain the business more fully but all Joyce could say was 'Look, I can see you're excited about it, but I'm not, and quite candidly, I can't see what there is to get excited about.' But by now her curiosity was aroused and a few days later she phoned Joe and asked 'Just how do you make money in this business?' Joe replied,'Joyce, just invite a few friends round to your house and let me come and talk to them.' 'What,' she asked 'to sell products to them?' 'No, to tell them about the business.' 'Is that all I have to do?' 'That's all—for now.' Joyce asked six couples to come and hear the enthusiastic American with his southern drawl. To her surprise three of them said they wanted to give Amway a try. When Al came in late that night he found a changed wife. She had opened the diary and booked every Thursday evening for Amway meetings.

That began a year of excitement and growth. Every week they showed the business to new people. Several of them joined. When they reached the fifteen percent level they went to an Amway seminar at York. That meeting was a turning point for Al. Until then he had left all the explaining to Joyce. He was quite unable to speak in public, and figures confused him. But at York he discovered that he was the only husband not doing business presentations. So he plucked up the courage. Joyce tells how she used to cringe as Al stumbled his way through the explanation and got the figures wrong but they had the enthusiasm and that was what counted. After ten months they became the first English Direct Distributors (only one month behind the Logans). The reaction was fantastic. As soon as the news was announced, the Greaves were inundated with letters and phone calls, congratulating them and asking them how they had done it. Soon they were organising rallies with the Logans and the Nellenbachs. In those early days when Amway was small there was a close cameraderie between all the leaders in the business. Much of the activity was in the Midlands. The Company headquarters were not far away at Milton Keynes, and, as Al said, 'the Company was fantastic—their back up and support in every way were superb'.

### *'King of the Nuts'*

My next port of call was an old-world cottage on the Yorkshire Wolds.

'I remember one American distributor saying to me, "I don't know how you build the business here. The British people are crazy. I'm going back to the States. Best of luck to you!"'

Dennis Peacock, a slim, moustached batchelor for whom the word 'dapper' might have been invented, sat by the brick inglenook in the time-weathered house where he lives with his father and gave me his impression of the early days of the Amway operation in Britain.

'I wouldn't wish them on anyone,' he said. 'Brian Hays told

me in America, "if you want a challenge, try to get Amway going in the UK."'

Dennis has not been in the business quite as long as the other pioneers I had already met but his angle on Amway UK's beginnings is interesting because he experienced the business first in the USA and then came back to north-east England to try to reproduce it in what was then virgin territory. Few would have assessed Dennis's prospects very highly when he left school at the age of nineteen, having laboriously accumulated six 'O' levels, certainly not his headmaster at one of England's prestigious public schools. His parents spent most of their lives abroad in the colonial service which was why their sons were educated in boarding school at home. Not knowing what else to do with himself, Dennis 'drifted into accountancy'. It took him eight years to qualify, mainly, he insists, because he was 'a slow learner'. 'Working smart had never been one of my attributes' he says. In 1973 he went to Florida to take up a position with an American company. He enjoyed the flashy cars and the impressive apartments but he increasingly hated accountancy and began to look for a business of his own because that seemed to be the way to the lifestyle he desired. And so he came across Amway. He was so excited by it that, as he says, 'I didn't sleep for a month'. This shiftless young man had, at last, found something he could commit himself to. He saved enough money not to have to work for a couple of years, learned all he could about Amway, and came home in 1976 to build a British Amway business.

Soon after his return, Dennis's mother contracted cancer. 'I shall always be grateful that I was able to be with her for the last six months of her life,' he says. The experience rocked him badly and added to the difficulties of running his business. Dennis knew that he would have to stay at home now to look after his father. That meant that Amway had to work. He felt very much on his own. He was virtually the only leading distributor in the whole north-east. His foster-sponsors, the Nellenbachs, had moved to Dublin within months of his arrival. Yet he was determined to succeed. He reached Direct Distributor level in a year (and was the first single person to do so). He built his group to over a hundred people. Then he tried a short cut—which turned out to be a dead end. He spent a great deal of time and money trying to persuade football clubs to join the Amway business as a means of fund-raising. The idea flopped because, as Dennis now realises, 'no-one will ever do this business unless they have a burning desire to do it for themselves and for what they want out of life.'

But despite this diversion Dennis's group was growing. Leaders were emerging. Other distributors were going Direct.

His faith was reaping its reward. New training programmes were introduced and soon flourishing centres existed in Humberside, Leeds, Nottingham, Middlesbrough and as far north as Morpeth in Northumberland. Nowadays the people of the north-east claim that theirs is one of the fastest developing organizations in the country. Hundreds of them hold Dennis Peacock in great esteem and affection and talk about his mad antics at rallies, his help in time of crisis, his boundless enthusiasm. They call him 'King Peacock' or, sometimes 'KP.—the King of the Nuts'. There was certainly a very enthusiastic cheer from one section of the 10,000 crowd in March 1982 when Dennis went on stage to receive his recognition as a new Emerald Direct distributor.

I pressed Dennis to tell me more about the problems of the early days.

'The basic problem was credibility,' he said. 'I remember having a run of thirty meetings and no-one joined. You see, what we had to offer was an American idea. The pyramid selling companies had recently been swindling a lot of people out of money. So when we came along with another marketing scheme from the USA people were naturally suspicious. Added to that, we had at that time no big success stories in this country.'

All that tied in with what other 'old-stagers' had told me. It was also supported by what appeared to be the prevalent attitude at Ada in the mid-1970s. In 1977 Charles Paul Conn in *The Possible Dream*, wrote of the concern felt at headquarters about the latest Amway subsidiary. Britain, he said, was regarded as 'a rather bleak market'. 'Even in the almost constantly optimistic atmosphere at Ada,' Conn observed, 'one detects a feeling that the development of Amway in England is expected to be slower than in other foreign areas.'

But Conn had not interviewed the people who *were* building the business in Britain. Now that I had met some of them I could see where the American writer had gone astray. He had forgotten the '*Mayflower* spirit'. In 1620, 102 'pilgrims', who passionately wanted to make a better future for themselves and their children set sail from England. I wonder how Conn would have assessed the chances of the precarious settlements they established on the eastern edge of his vast continent. They must have seemed 'rather bleak' in the early years. Certainly, their progress could be expected to be 'slower than in other foreign areas'. Today the United States of America only exists because of the patience, determination, courage and total faith of those pioneer settlers. It has been the same with Amway's growth in this country—a few dedicated pioneers with total belief in the business have established a highly successful marketing operation in Britain.

*Nothing succeeds like success*

'We could see that Amway was working, and working very well for people in the States and we didn't believe that the British were basically different. So what was needed was for a few people here to be really successful. That would encourage others and lead to real growth. The turning point came for me when I decided to make it work and to lead by example.'

Jenny Smith was talking to me in the lounge of her lovely old cottage in a Gloucestershire village. She and Geoff are known throughout the international Amway network as trail blazers of the British business. They were, in fact, the first Diamond Direct distributors, and have been in the business since October 1973.

Geoff recalls how he left school as a lad with big ideas, few qualifications, little talent and no money. He dreamed of a big house with a swimming pool and two or three sports cars in the garage. But the dream was far from the reality for a fifteen-pound-a-week builder's labourer. However, Geoff did have one qualification—determination to succeed. Within a few years he had established his own business as a plastering contractor. By this time he had met and married Jenny and they lived in a semi-detached house in Gloucester. For years they had to survive on Jenny's income, as a schools' career officer because most of Geoff's earnings had to be ploughed back into the business. It was an old friend of Jenny's who introduced them to Amway. They could see that this fellow was excited and when he told Geoff that he could retire and enjoy complete freedom by the time he was thirty, the twenty-three-year-old plasterer began to catch some of the excitement himself.

Being, as Geoff says, ambitious people, they started on the business enthusiastically, devoting to it as much free time as they could spare. This was, by no means easy, as Geoff had to go out pricing jobs in the evenings and Jenny was studying for a higher qualification in her profession. 'I don't believe anyone can say he is too busy for Amway,' Geoff reflected. 'If someone wants to do this business, he'll find the time to do it. Time was certainly no problem for us.' Nor was Geoff put off by his total lack of public speaking. 'In this business,' he said 'you very quickly learn how to take meetings and, anyway, our sponsor took our first few meetings for us. I practised presenting the plan by speaking into a tape recorder. When I meet people now who are hesitant about joining Amway because they are shy or reserved I can honestly tell them that they'll overcome that through the system.'

Geoff and Jenny reached Direct distributor level in twenty months. 'That was pretty good, for the early days, although, of course, people are doing it a lot quicker now,' Geoff observed in his quiet, country voice. He recalled how the Americans like to refer to the 'malaise anglais'—the English disease—but that was something he totally dismissed. He reckoned that the impact of pyramid selling had been considerable and that the British people wanted to see some success in this country before they would commit themselves. Jenny added that another difficulty had been the limited nature of the product range. At the beginning, distributors only had seventeen products to show people.

Geoff said that it was 1976–7 that their own business and the fortunes of Amway in the UK took a dramatic upturn. Company representatives sat down with the leading distributors to analyse the situation and hammer out a new strategy (see below pp. 21). 'What George Howden, who came over from Ada, really made clear to us was that it was *our* business and that the Company was there to help us, not to tell us what to do. We established a new kind of harmony between the Company and the distributor organisation which has existed ever since. We began to run our own training programmes and rallies and things started to take off.' Another stimulus to them was their first trip to the USA. When Geoff and Jenny saw the kind of lifestyle American distributors were enjoying it boosted the credibility of the organization and gave them a new determination.

I was interested to discover what the Smiths had learned from their American contacts. Was the business different on this side of the Atlantic? Did it need adapting for the 'stiff-upper-lip' English? Were we less enthusiastic over here? Less materialistic? Geoff and Jenny were convinced that there was no basic difference in the business and that British people were just as capable of enthusiasm as their American cousins. But Jenny weighed my questions carefully. 'Of course, there are cultural differences. The British don't stand on chairs and demonstrate their enthusiasm as wildly as the Americans. We're probably more reserved about making the first move; for instance in speaking to strangers. But once that first move is made, people respond very quickly. As to materialism, I'm not sure. We certainly don't have the same standard of material prosperity here and that probably leads most people to settle for less. But I'm quite convinced that Amway works just as well in Britain and that people can get from it what they want, whether its material reward or not.'

That led on naturally to the question 'What have *you* got out of it'. 'One of the nice things about this business is that it is stable. You reach a point sooner or later when it goes on without you,' Geoff said. 'That happened to us in 1977 and it was then that I began to wind down the plastering business. So, the first big thing Amway has given us is freedom. Another big thrill for me was going out and buying the Mercedes, which was the car I had always wanted. Then again there's the travel. We can go where we want, when we want. Our second USA trip was for a month and we capped it by spending a week in Hawaii. And all that is down to Amway. Before we got into this business we were leading ordinary lives.' Jenny took up the point enthusiastically. 'Yes, before, we were small-thinkers. Now, we think big. We know anything can happen because so many things have happened. There's all the travel ... and having someone in to clean my house. That's perhaps a small thing but I remember the kick it gave me when we were able to afford that. But perhaps the biggest thing Amway has given me is more self-confidence.'

Reaching the Diamond level was obviously one of the achievements that boosted the Smiths' self-confidence. But more important they believe, was the impact that had on the organisation. It showed people that it could be done and other distributors very soon followed. Now their sights are set on Double Diamond and beyond; not, as Geoff says, because they need the money (they already enjoy a very substantial five figure income), but because they want to encourage others. 'After all,' he added, 'nothing succeeds like success.'

### *Drawing the threads together*

I felt I now had enough information to explain and assess the establishment of the amazing Amway phenomenon in Great Britain.

It had begun in 1973 and it would be difficult to imagine a less auspicious year. 1973 was the year of the great oil crisis and the start of hyper-inflation. When OPEC put up the price of crude, the cost of all goods which have to be manufactured and transported began to 'escalate' (a newly coined verb destined to become one of the most overworked in the English language). Trade unions negotiated large wage increases to preserve their members' living standards. Pay and prices chased each other round in a rising spiral and soon inflation had soared to 21%. The effect on British morale was shattering. For the first time since 1945 the vision of an ever-brightening future evaporated. Up until then few people had doubted that their living standards would continue to improve, however slowly. Through rising salaries, hire purchase arrangements and credit cards, families could slowly accumulate material assets—a second car, a bigger home, a freezer, holidays abroad, colour television, etc. Now the situation changed rapidly. The later seventies were years of industrial unrest, factories working at half capacity, bankruptcies and rising unemployment. Individuals reacted in various ways. Some thought that the answer was to take money away from the rich and successful and give it to the poor and unsuccessful: they called this 'redistribution of wealth'. Some 'opted out of the rat race', retiring into the country to rediscover the 'simple life', practise 'self-sufficiency' and 'do their own thing' (all clichés which have become hallmarks of the seventies). Middle-aged men swapped careers. An increasing number of young couples, uncertain of the future, rejected the convention of marriage. People began to cut their coat according to their cloth. They stopped trying to keep up with the Joneses. They talked more about the 'quality of life' and less about the 'standard of living'. To insulate themselves against disappointment, they stopped wanting material things. As Joyce Greaves says 'people forgot how to dream'.

It was hardly a favourable socio-economic climate in which to propagate a totally new business concept. When enthusiastic Amway distributors went to their friends and neighbours with a business proposition as yet untried in this country they met, in many cases, dazed apathy and disbelief. Amway was a unique concept and those who had it explained to them tended to judge it in terms of other business operations which they knew and could understand. Some, like Joyce Greaves, thought at first that it was just a way of retailing soap, like any other direct sales operation. Others believed it was pyramid selling. The heyday of the pyramid companies, was the eight years 1965–73, and in that brief span they caused a great deal of misery. They worked like this: an agent arrived in a new area and filled a warehouse with his products—products which were usually of a high standard. He advertised locally and held a series of meetings. At these he used a well-prepared and persuasive sales pitch to induce people to invest hundreds or thousands of pounds in batches of goods. The more they bought, the cheaper the price. All they, in their turn, had to do, according to the pyramid salesman, was offload smaller quantities onto a few friends at an increased price. The friends would break down the consignment still further, taking their profit, and so on, down the pyramid. A few people who got in at the top and who had an aptitude for selling made a killing. The rest were taken for a ride. MPs, consumer organisations, the press and television companies were inundated with heartrending stories of people who had invested their savings in expensive training and goods they could not sell either because they lacked real expertise or because they were so far down the pyramid that there was no more profit to be extracted from the merchandise. What usually happened at this stage was that the original super-salesmen reappeared, offering to take the stock off their hands at a fraction of the original cost. The 1973 Fair Trading Act outlawed pyramid selling. By then most people knew someone who had been caught in one of these operations and they were very wary of any other American marketing schemes. Those who took the trouble to look at Amway with its impeccable moral and legal standards soon discovered that any similarity to pyramid selling was purely superficial. No Amway distributor invests capital in stock. Both distributors and customers are protected by the full money back guarantee. Goods do not increase in price when they change hands. All distributors pay the same amount for goods (its called the distributor deposit), no matter how many levels of the business those goods have passed through, and there is a suggested customer price which is not exceeded. As Lynn Faulds-Wood acknowledged in a *Daily Mail* article (29 January 1980), Amway's rules 'require perfect paragon-like standards of frankness, honesty, integrity and responsibility'.

There was another, deeper, resistance that had to be overcome and that was an innate suspicion among many British people of anything American. There is no doubt that a cultural barrier exists between British and American people, paradoxically because our cultures are so close. When two objects are very similar, their differences are more obvious. For example, the same language is spoken on both sides of the Atlantic. For this very reason we are acutely aware of the American accent, of linguistic differences ('gas' and 'petrol', 'sidewalk' and 'pavement', etc), and minute changes of usage. The same is true across the cultural spectrum; Britons and Americans dress differently, behave differently in company, furnish their homes differently, etc. Mingled with this was a certain resentment, having its roots in the Second World War and its aftermath. It was commonly said in the 1940s that US servicemen had, three faults; they were 'over-paid, over-sexed and over here'. For twenty or thirty years after 1945 Britain was conscious of being the 'poor relation', often patronised by and always jealous of Uncle Sam. Prejudice gives rise to myth. Just as the popular American concept of the Englishman was that of a bowler-hatted, reserved, class-ridden snob, so most Britons' picture of an American salesman was of a man in a loud suit, rimless spectacles and a plastic grin, practising the hard sell. Hugh Hofton, another British Amway pioneer, recalled going to his first Amway meeting in 1973. 'A person advanced across the room with his hand outstretched. This person wore a check jacket and check trousers and the checks didn't match. He grabbed my hand and bellowed, "Hi!".

And I thought, "no way am I getting involved in this business, whatever it is".'

The pioneer distributors, therefore, had to develop a distinctive British style for Amway, and that took time. The Greaves told me how they had to tone down the rallies. In the States large meetings (often numbering many thousands of distributors) are run on showbiz lines. Bands, singers and dancers are used to create an atmosphere. Speakers are given massive build-ups by comperes, and audiences respond with hoots, cheers and whistles. Americans expect to display their enthusiasm openly and they expect to have that enthusiasm channelled, organised. Consider, for example, the razamataz that attends state and federal elections or the teams of gorgeous girls who perform cheerleading routines at footbal and baseball matches. Over here we do things rather differently and our transatlantic cousins find it difficult to understand us. One American distributor who had begun to grasp the difference put it this way: 'When I want to know whether an Englishman is getting excited, I watch his eyebrows'. It is not that we are incapable of enthusiasm or that we dislike showing it—go to any football match on a Saturday afternoon and you will see plenty of wild, sometimes violent, displays. The point is that we allow ourselves fewer outlets for it. If we want to indulge in exuberant expressions of feelings we congregate at race tracks, pop concerts, boxing matches and sporting contests. We do not associate such activity with the more 'serious' aspects of life—religion, politics, business. That is why we are the despair of fanatics and demagogues. Contrived enthusiasm—so natural in American Amway rallies—could only be counterproductive here. Even the style of the *Amagram*, the company's in-house magazine, had to be muted. Joyce Greaves, for example, suggested to the general manager that 'Hi there!' was not the best way to greet British people through its pages. By the very nature of the business these large problems had to be faced up to by a small number of relatively inexperienced distributors.

Very close personal links existed between individuals and the top management at Milton Keynes. Amway (UK) Ltd gave every possible help to distributors (usually in the way of providing speakers and organising meetings), and from time to time spokesmen came over from the parent company to provide inspiration and practical assistance. But essentially the staff of Amway were pledged not to interfere in the development of the British distributor organisation. That meant that, for three or four years, there were pockets of people all over the country running their Amway businesses in their own way. Most of them had been sponsored from abroad, received little help from 'upline' and had little technical knowhow to pass on 'downline'. At the end of 1978 Don and Angie Nellenbach left to set up home in Eire and to start all over again building a third Amway business from the bottom (their UK business reached Emerald level early in 1979). The Logans returned to the States a few months later to move into a magnificent new home in California (from where they visit their English friends once a year). The challenge was, therefore, now, with the British organization to develop its own leadership.

Important steps had already been taken to set up the UK operation on a sounder footing. Earlier in 1976 George Howden (now affectionately referred to as St George by some of his British friends) came over from Ada to co-ordinate this activity. John Dodds was promoted to general manager, and was to guide Amway (UK) Ltd through the next important five years. Stewart McArthur (who later took over as general manager) was brought onto the staff. The Company pledged itself, as well as providing products and product information, to helping the distributor organization in a variety of ways such as holding regional rallies and business expansion seminars, while the distributor organisation was responsible fully for developing training programmes and business building patterns. It was from this point that growth began to accelerate.

Nothing can take away from the grit, determination and sheer 'stickability' of the early distributors but other factors did come to their aid in the late 1970s. As world-wide recession deepened, apathy and depression gave way—at least among the more resilient and positive members of the community—to an eagerness to seek other means of earning money. As employment prospects became less secure and the profitability of private business dwindled, people of all kinds—wage-earners, salaried staff, self-employed, professionals, businessmen, skilled, semi-skilled and unskilled workers—began to be impressed by a marketing operation which was actually expanding and expanding dramatically (International turnover, which had stood at half a million dollars in the first year of business was, by 1977 approaching the $500,000,000 level and UK activity was beginning to follow the same pattern).

At the same time that the British character of Amway UK was emerging there was a general movement in the country towards closer links with the USA. Sir Freddie Laker pioneered cheap transatlantic flights. Places like Miami, which had been the exclusive playground of wealthy Americans now became, to use Dennis Peacock's phrase, 'the Butlins of the USA', at least in the off-season. The trend of tourism was reversed; more Britons went to America and fewer Americans came to Britain. In place of prejudice there grew a realisation of how Americans really live, an understanding of sales and business methods 'over there', and an appreciation of what free enterprise can mean in a country where individual initiative is actively encouraged.

More and more distributors visited their counterparts in the USA and explored the techniques employed in the parent country. They brought back with them ideas, books and cassette tapes to help them build their British businesses. More important than the training schemes and new methods they applied was the philosophy to which they exposed themselves and the members of their organisation, a philosophy expressed in the books and tapes widely used in America and, now, throughout Britain. The philosophy may be called positive thinking. Works such as David J Schwartz's *Magic of Thinking Big*, Norman Vincent Peale's *Power of Positive Thinking* and Dale Carnegie's *How to Win Friends and Influence People*, have been big sellers in North America for years and the philosophy behind them has made a considerable impact. These books have been known in this country, too, but they have had little influence. In some circles they have even been regarded with mild amusement. But British Amway people rapidly began to realise that the ideals of self-confidence, enthusiasm and concern for others that the books and tapes set forth were the ideals on which Amway was founded and, therefore, the only ones which would make it work properly.

The same is true of cassette tapes. For example, a set of tapes called, simply, *Attitude* by Skip Ross, one of the most dynamic and witty public speakers in the USA, has had probably more impact on Amway's expansion than any other single aid. Joyce Greaves recalled how she came across the Skip Ross tapes almost by accident when browsing through a collection owned by an American distributor. Her reaction on listening was 'This is magic'. The Greaves realised that they and many people in their organisation needed to hear the Skip Ross message, 'Believe in yourself and you can achieve whatever you want to achieve'. They circulated copies. Hugh Hofton heard one and started using it in his organisation. Soon most of the big groups were using it and its effects certainly were 'magic'. Dennis Peacock says that in his organisation it led to a 'terrific explosion of growth'. When British distributors were able to sit down in their own homes and hear the Amway millionaires talking about their experiences and analysing how they got where they were, they were inspired to go all out for success, especially when Skip Ross convinced them 'you can do it'.

*The machine*

Now, the situation could hardly be more different from that of the early years. In 1981 membership was up by 190% on 1980 and sales had increased by 175%. Amway has 'arrived' in the UK and is destined to be a permanent part of our way of life. Not only that, its commercial and social impact will increase throughout the years ahead. If any event may be said to symbolise this new permanence it is the opening of the four million pound office and warehouse complex at Tongwell in September 1982. (See pp. 83 f. below.)

But buildings are cold bricks and mortar. To grasp what Amway is really all about you need to go to the annual convention, the largest gathering of Amway people in Britain. In 1981 just under 5,000 people were present. A year later the event drew 10,000 to the National Exhibition Arena in Birmingham, one of the largest indoor centres in the country. It was, as a matter of interest, the biggest Amway event ever staged outside the USA—a striking vindication of those pioneers who had refused to accept the gloomy forecasts offered by some critics only a few years before. Distributors from all over the United Kingdom arrived there in cars and coachloads. Many had risen long before dawn to start the journey. There were Direct distributors bringing their groups whose members chattered happily together as old friends do and greeted each other with hugs and kisses. Inside the packed hall home-made banners and placards proclaimed the areas represented. Groups identified with each other as coming from the same region or being part of the same line of sponsorship. And that cheerful, excited crowd was the world of Amway in microcosm. It was rather like the complex workings of a clock. Each group was a cog made up of several teeth which were its distributors. Each cog had contact with one or more of its neighbours. Some were large, some were small, and they moved at different speeds. But because all this diversity was harmonised the mechanism operated smoothly and efficiently.

Yet the analogy of a machine gives a cold, impersonal impression, as though all these people were being manipulated to serve some purely commercial end. No-one present at the Birmingham convention, or any other Amway rally or meeting I have been to could possibly come away with that impression. In a corner of the arena I spoke with Jerry Milverton, a cheerful man in his thirties, cheerful despite being confined to a wheelchair by a serious spinal injury which gives him frequent bouts of pain.

'For the first time in my life I feel I belong to a family—and what a family!' He waved his hand round the packed rows of seats. 'I was an orphan, a Barnardo's boy. I never had a family—till now.'

As if to emphasise the point, a young couple came up and joined in the conversation, and then an older man. I edged away and left Jerry enjoying his Amway 'cousins'. All the people in that vast crowd felt they belonged to something—something big and worthwhile. The fostering of group identity and, through the group, identity with the whole is of paramount importance. New distributors now attend a short course of training run by their sponsors or Direct distributors. These sessions bring together dozens, scores or, in some cases, hundreds, of new distributors. They come to learn about the business but the very fact of being together with so many other beginners gives them a sense of belonging and fosters a corporate loyalty to the leaders. When they have completed their training, distributors are encouraged to return bringing their own new recruits with them. In this way the information is passed downline without becoming distorted in the process. From the groups, distributors travel to regional and national meetings. The business expansion programmes, designed to show those who had made a start in Amway how they could move rapidly to the higher levels, which the company started in 1977 were phased out as soon as all the leading distributors had set up their own 'higher training' programmes and seminars.

Nowadays an active Amway distributor's calendar is chock full of events, some business functions, some social, mostly a bit of both. Everyone believes that Amway should be fun. The levels of achievement are milestones on the road to success. They are also pointers to the glittering lifestyle many distributors aspire to. As soon as a couple 'go Direct' they are invited to a two-day seminar in a luxury hotel. In between wining and dining and exchanging news with each other, there are opportunities to see the warehouse complex at Milton Keynes, hear the company's plans for the future, and share ideas on business development. Soon afterwards these couples will qualify for the Annual Leadership Seminar.

This is a highlight of the year for every Direct Distributor and above. For seven days they live in luxury as guests of the company in some Mediterranean sun spot. Even for seasoned travellers, the VIP treatment they receive is impressive; for those not accustomed to stylish holidays abroad the experience is very exciting indeed. I vividly remember Barbara Rigg, a petite, vivacious Mancunian, sitting on the floor of her new home and hugging her knees as she bubbled enthusiastically about her first visit to Spain. 'We were met at the airport and escorted to the plane.

People took care of our passports and baggage. It was unbelievable—really.' She giggled. 'We felt like royalty ... Then, when we landed, I had to get Dennis to pinch me. I said "This can't be happening to us". We went everywhere that week—coach excursions, and shopping trips, and dinners, dances, parties. ... Oh, it was fabulous. And, of course, we learned an enormous amount about the business. We were shattered when we got back.'

As distributors scale the ladder of success above the Direct level they slip, by degrees, into the way of life they had previously only read about in the gossip columns: star billing when they speak at rallies; periodic visits to their counterparts in other countries; invitations to visit Ada and travel around the USA: fabulous dinner parties to celebrate their arrival at Emerald and Diamond levels; and when they have reached Diamond they become part of the Diamond Forum.

This meets twice a year, once at a premier British hotel and once at one of the more exclusive European venues, such as the Hotel de Paris, Monaco. There, the leaders of the distributor organisation meet with corporate executives to discuss business matters of mutual interest—and to enjoy themselves. British leaders at Double Diamond level form part of the international Executive Diamond Council which convenes annually in Switzerland, the Bahamas or some other attractive resort. For all these events Amway Corporation picks up the bill.

This lifestyle is one which most participants would never have envisaged themselves enjoying a few years ago. It was Barbara Rigg, again, who told me with unconcealed excitement, 'We feel as though we've just got on a dream train—and we're not going to get off!' It is a lifestyle into which, as I said, distributors slip by degrees. For most ordinary people the experience of sunning on the deck of a luxury yacht, being whisked around America by private jet, or dining in the world's most exclusive restaurants could only happen to them as a consequence of some sudden stroke of good fortune, such as winning the football pools. The problem with instant wealth is that its recipients often cannot fully enjoy it because they lack the confidence and poise to go with it. But in Amway people seem to grow in stature as their income rises. I recall Robert Hayward an Emerald Direct distributor in Manchester telling me of his wife's appalling shyness before they entered the business. She had few friends and for her the prospect of meeting new people was so terrifying that hours before a social engagement she would be physically sick. Now Suzanne will happily talk to a hall full of hundreds of people and another distributor described her admiringly to me as 'a complete lady'. Of course, there is also another reason why these ordinary people enjoy life at the top; they have the satisfaction of knowing that they've worked for it and that they deserve their success.

Not everyone in Amway aspires to the jet set image. People have different motives for joining Amway. Dennis Peacock, for instance, looks forward with eager anticipation to a life centred around private aeroplanes, fast cars and frequent visits to exotic resorts. By contrast Al and Joyce Greaves also enjoy foreign travel but appreciate much more their freedom and the simple, quiet life they live in 'the house that Amway bought'. It is of immense value for them to know that whatever happens to them their sons' futures are secure, for they will inherit an Amway Diamond income and will be able to build the business on if they wish. 'It's changed our lives completely,' says Al, 'and we're very grateful. This house is a case in point.' He told me how they had been out for a drive one afternoon when suddenly Joyce had pointed excitedly out of the window 'That's the house I want!' she shouted. 'Don't be daft, woman. It's sold.' Al pointed to the board in the front garden. 'I don't care, I want it.' From that moment the smart house set in its own grounds became for Joyce 'our house'. The saga of how the Greaves were eventually able to buy it is a long one. Some would call it a sequence of coincidences. They call it positive thinking.

Then again, there are many people in the distributor organisation who have no wish to reach the upper levels. They have joined to earn a few hundred or a few thousand a year. They want to be sure the mortgage is covered or pay for a good annual holiday. Everyone in Amway is on his own dream train, and it will always stop at the destination he has chosen.

CHAPTER 3

# A Casket of Jewels

EMERALDS! Pearls! Diamonds! Rubies!

What dazzling images the words conjure up. Yet, in the world of Amway they have other, though scarcely less dazzling, meanings. They represent some of the levels attainable in the business by distributors. They are like the rungs of a ladder reaching from the ground to the millionaire's penthouse. It is a very skilfully constructed ladder, for although it may be difficult for the novice to see the top clearly, he can set his feet firmly on the lower rungs and he knows that the top is there to be reached. It is up to him how quickly he climbs but as long as he goes on raising one foot above the other he will reach the level he has set himself to reach, the level corresponding to the income which will enable him to realise his dreams.

The ladder is set squarely before the gaze of everyone who, however hesitantly, embarks on a career in Amway. He is shown that at every stage he will receive recognition of his achievements and incentives will be set before him encouraging him to reach higher. The first goal of the serious distributor is to reach the 21% bonus level. In attaining this he will have gathered a group (probably) of between 60 and 100 people, generating, perhaps, £3,500 in business volume per month. (It is difficult to be precise about figures since stock prices increase with inflation. However, the system is so constructed that the volume of stock units moved to qualify a distributor for the next level remains constant.) When he holds this level for three consecutive months he becomes a Direct distributor. All his dealings will now be 'directly' with the Company and not via a sponsor. In effect, 'going Direct' sorts out the men from the boys, those who intend to take Amway seriously from those who are unable or unwilling to put in the necessary amount of creative energy. Direct distributors are the building blocks of Amway. And the rewards for reaching this level? A Direct distributor receives a 21% bonus on his total group volume. Even by the time he has paid a proportion of this to his 'downline' distributors he will have a healthy income derived from a part-time business. At this stage of his Amway career the distributor will already feel himself to be part of a widespread social/business network. Since mutual help is of the essence of the Amway operation, he will have greatly enlarged his circle of friends. He will be attending meetings and rallies 'upline' and will have begun to organise his own. Every October he will probably attend the leadership seminar and bask in the Mediterranean sun with other Direct distributors. How long does it take to reach this level? There can be no precise answer to that question, since every distributor sets his own pace. From my own experience of the British organisation, however, I can say that the average seems to lie somewhere between six and eighteen months with a tendency towards the shorter period as national momentum increases.

As our new Direct distributor reaches for the higher rungs on the ladder he will discover that, for the most part, qualification rests upon helping others to achieve what he has achieved—Direct distributorship. This is called, in the Amway jargon, 'breaking Directs'. The more Directs he has in his own organisation, the higher he goes. For example, he reaches the Emerald level when he has sponsored three Direct 'legs' for six months in a fiscal year (a leg is another term for a line of sponsorship) and he reaches the Diamond level when he has sponsored six Direct 'legs' for six months in a fiscal year. We can perhaps explain this best with a much simplified diagram.

The Amway levels above Direct distributor are, in ascending order: Ruby, Pearl, Emerald, Diamond, Double Diamond, Triple Diamond, Crown, Crown Ambassador. Every level carries additional cash bonuses and incentives. It is not possible to tie these levels to specific income brackets but I have observed that distributors who wish to give up their conventional jobs tend to do so at the Pearl or Emerald level (Amway strongly dissuade anyone from 'going full time' until he has a strong business possibly at the Emerald level). Crowns and Crown Ambassadors can earn six-figure incomes.

But is it really true that *anyone* can reach these dizzy heights? Can Mr or Mrs Average, the fellow next door, the person reading this book, can anyone who wants to become an Amway millionaire? That was the question I was constantly asking myself as I toured Britain talking to Amway distributors. It became obvious very early on that there were people—plenty of them—making their fortunes with the help of this organisation but that fact proved little. Perhaps these successful distributors were the sort of people who would have made it to the top whatever they chose to do. Perhaps Al and Joyce Greaves, for all that they seemed very down-to-earth folk, were really a couple with hidden fires which would have been fanned by something else if Amway had not come along first. In a sense, I hoped that was true. It would make for a more credible story. If you write a book which says

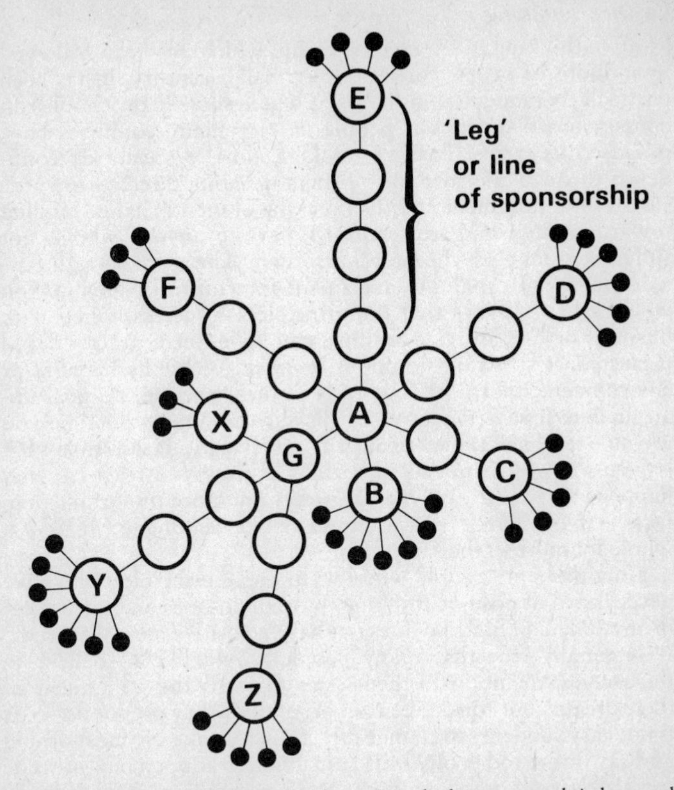


Here we have a Diamond Direct distributor (A) who has sponsored six legs, each of which is at the 21% level and contains Direct distributors (B,C,D,E,F,G) (G) is, in fact, an Emerald Direct distributor because he has sponsored three legs, each of which is at the 21% level or above, with Direct distributors, X,Y,Z.

'Here is a simple idea which anyone can follow and get rich' it is rather like publishing a 'true' account of little green men getting out of a flying saucer. You run the risk of being dubbed a sensation-monger or simply a crank. So I questioned my interviewees as closely as I could. I probed the workings of the organisation, looking for flaws. Whether or not what I discovered adds up to a foolproof system the reader must decide. But there is one important principle I found operating in every thriving Amway group, so it may be helpful to isolate and examine it before we go any further. It is called 'positive thinking'.

*Positive Thinking*

Positive thinking is an attitude to life which has been followed by millions of people for more than half a century. It has been particularly influential in the USA, where some high schools run courses based on it, but people in very many countries have practised its tenets. Positive thinking aims to create self-confidence through the forming of mental habits directed towards success and fulfilment and the breaking of mental habits tending towards failure and frustration. It says to anyone who is not suffering from a psychological disorder, 'There are enough buried reserves of capability and talent for you to be anyone you want to be.'* It says that the principles of success, whether in business or human relationships, can be learned, practised and perfected. It says that no-one is branded for life by heredity or environment, that no difficulty is insurmountable, no goal unattainable. It says that if you believe something is possible you are nine tenths of the way towards achieving it. It says that what happens to you is not as important as how you react to what happens to you. It says that attitudes are more important than facts—'if life hands you a lemon, make lemonade'. It says a whole lot more in the same vein.

Now there are people who live by these principles who have never heard of positive thinking. Indeed, no-one can be a success in any sphere of life who does not have a positive mental attitude. It is equally true that many people would like to believe in themselves, to motivate themselves towards the attainment of their dreams but for one reason or another they do not do so. It is not easy suddenly to change direction; to wake up one morning and say 'From today onwards I am going to adopt a new attitude towards myself, my wife, my job, my neighbours'. Old failures, old prejudices, old misunderstandings cling like magnets and it requires perseverance and dedication to pluck them off one by one. But to find some new area of life where the principles of positive thinking can be applied, where you can experiment, as it were, with a new approach, that is a different matter.

And Amway seems to fill the bill very neatly for many people. It presents them with a pattern of business success that obviously works. The new distributor can believe in Amway because of its proven record. The only other ingredient he requires is belief in himself. That is where positive thinking comes in. Within the distributor organisation popular books and cassette tapes on motivation and the development of self-confidence are recommended and circulated. The majority of people use them and apparently to

* Daniel C. Steere, *I am—I Can.*

good effect. The man or woman who can say 'Amway works and I am going to make it work for me' is set fair to succeed.

*Building an Amway business—the routine*

It is easy to describe how a typical Amway business is built because the pattern is clearly defined. Moreover everyone in the organisation is doing the same things. Those at the higher levels work in exactly the same way as the newest recruit. Of course, it is true in Amway as in anything else, that nothing succeeds like success. Distributors who have already built up strong organisations and good incomes have the additional credibility and confidence to enable them to grow faster but the fact remains that the techniques used and the information required are the same for the Crown Ambassador as they are for the beginner.

Let's think of a couple (we will call them Dave and Shirley) being introduced to the world of Amway by an existing distributor. This will be done at a 'sponsoring meeting'. This is an occasion when the sales and marketing plan is explained and some products shown either to a group of interested people or to just one or two. Because of the way business growth is usually illustrated on a blackboard or on sheets of paper this demonstration is sometimes called 'showing the circles'.

When Dave and Shirley decide to 'give it a try' they will be invited to do three things; arrange their own first sponsoring meeting, attend training sessions and buy the Company's starter kit (it will be explained to them that the cost of the kit is refundable should they decide to change their minds) containing information about Amway and its products, as well as order forms, an application form and other paperwork. The person who invited them now becomes their 'sponsor' and will help them get established. This will initially involve taking one or more of their early sponsoring meetings. Probably with some trepidation Dave and Shirley invite a number of friends and neighbours to their home to hear about 'a part time business'. As a result of that meeting probably some people will sign up. Others may not wish to join but may ask to try some of the products. In this way our two distributors acquire those two categories of people essential to their business—new distributors and customers.

Dave and Shirley now become sponsors to the people who have joined their group. They will take meetings for them (though their own sponsor may help them to work 'downline' for a time). Dave and Shirley may order products via their sponsor or, if they live more than fifteen miles from their sponsor, direct from the Amway warehouse (there are weekly deliveries to all parts of the country). Similarly, their distributors may order from them or not. Dave and Shirley will take members of their group along to the training sessions organised by their 'upline' or sponsor and occasionally to larger functions such as rallies and conventions. At rallies they will meet hundreds of other people like themselves, hear speeches by successful distributors and see awards presented to those who have reached upper levels. By this time Dave and Shirley will find their enthusiasm and excitement growing as they feel themselves becoming part of the world of Amway and as they enjoy helping others in their group to grow. The finances of the organisation work very simply. Every month Shirley and Dave receive a cheque from their sponsor. They bank it and send smaller cheques to their immediate distributors (who, in turn, do the same). They will probably arrange social functions with their group. The 'pot-luck' party, to which every guest contributes a bottle and a food dish, seems to be a great favourite in Amway.

Before they reach the Direct level Shirley and Dave will probably help to run training meetings or they may find that their group is so large that they need to arrange their own training sessions. The time will come when they are running their own small rallies. As their business grows, therefore, they receive not only more recognition and more incentive but also more responsibility for those downline. If they are the sort of people who respond to these impulses their business will grow steadily and they will enjoy the world of Amway. If they are by nature more hesitant they will probably reach the point at which they have to take stock of their situation. Many top level distributors described to me such a time of decision. One couple explained that their business took off when 'we stopped giving Amway all we'd got and began giving it all it takes'.

This 'moment of truth' is so important for many successful Amway people that it is worth examining closely. Let us assume that Dave and Shirley have made a good start. That target Direct distributor level is almost within reach. But they cannot quite seem to attain it. They sit down one evening at the kitchen table and try to sort things out. They know by now that they can attain their dreams within the world of Amway. It is up to them. They have to improve their performance. Perhaps they need to devote more time to sponsoring, or to helping some of their less able distributors. Perhaps they need to work at creating a warmer environment. Perhaps the training programme needs revising. Perhaps their group needs stronger contact with people 'upline'. Whatever Dave and Shirley decide and whatever action they take will involve their moving to a deeper level of commitment, to developing traits of character hitherto dormant or not very active. This is obviously what Amway people mean when they talk about the importance of 'personal development'. It explains why shy people lose their shyness, why withdrawn people learn how to make friends, why uncertain people become confident. Anyone who is determined to succeed in this business will change in the process of succeeding.

Does this mean that Amway produces a stereotype? Not in my experience, although there are certainly characteristics which all successful distributors share in differing degrees. They are friendly, cheerful, optimistic. They know where they are going and are confident of their ability to get there. They have a real concern for Amway and everyone in it. Since none of us can keep the various parts of our life in separate watertight compartments, these attitudes colour all their relationships and activities. One Diamond distributor said to me, 'If Amway packed up tomorrow I know that I could go out and conquer the world in some other capacity.'

It is part of the Amway magic that those who persevere remain loyal to the pattern. There is nothing compelling them to do so. They are all independent. When they sign an application form to become distibutors they only commit themselves to observing the Amway code of ethics and rules of conduct. These cover such matters as not making false claims, being courteous and prompt when dealing with customers, not selling products through shop or other retail outlets, etc. Providing they abide by these simple rules, no-one has any legal hold over them—not the Company, not the distributor organisation, not their sponsor. They can do as they please. For example, there is nothing to stop a distributor going out and selling products door-to-door. Some have, in fact, done so, but they tend not to stick. The reason is partly financial. Trying to work Amway as though it were a conventional, discount-based, direct selling exercise simply does not bring people the rewards that are available to those who 'follow the pattern'. There is, however, more to it than that. Within the world of Amway there is generated a sense of interdependence and mutual concern. Distributors are urged to follow the lead of those above them in their line of sponsorship. This leads to subtle distinctions and differences of emphasis between the organisations headed by some of the leaders but these are minimal within the overall Amway scheme of things.

Let us return to Dave and Shirley. The day they receive their 'DD' pins is a big one for them. It happens at a rally in front of several hundred Amway people. Their own group has turned out in force to cheer as they go up on stage for a hug and a kiss and a word of congratulation from their sponsor. Soon after there follows a two-day gathering for new Directs at Milton Keynes, where they meet the top executives of the Company, tour the headquarters, and enjoy luxury hotel accommodation and special meals. Everything is geared to making them feel that they are now an important part of the organisation, as, indeed, they are. The next event they have their sights on is the Leadership Travel Seminar, the annual gathering of all the top UK distributors in, let us say, Ibiza. By the time they have returned from a week soaking up sun and Amway inspiration they have begun to experience and develop an appreciation for the high life. It may occur to our imaginary couple now, if it has not already done so, that Amway is the part of their life they enjoy the most. Dave's electronics firm now seems very tame by comparison and Shirley cannot wait to give up her secretarial job. Their evening and weekend activities in Amway bring them together in a joint enterprise which is creative and fun. They plan how they can quickly build their business to the point where their Amway income at least equals their current joint salaries. They attend business development seminars organised for Amway leaders. They spend time with their own more determined distributors. The day comes when they are standing on a platform handing out DD pins to Paul and Jean, a couple in one of their 'legs' who have long since become close personal friends. Now they know they are on their way to Pearl, Emerald, Diamond and beyond.

Let us take our last look at Shirley and Dave eighteen months later. The scene is a private room in a smart local hotel. There is a dinner in progress for about twenty people. The Company are the hosts. Shirley and Dave are the guests of honour. They have recently been awarded their Emerald pins amidst emotional scenes at a national convention in front of thousands of distributors. This is a quieter, more intimate way of saying 'Congratulations'. Dave and Shirley have come a long way in the last few months. Their group has grown to such a size that they cannot possibly know everyone in it. They now have financial independence and no longer have to work for someone else. The alarm clock has gone into early retirement. Soon they will be moving into a new house. The baby who is on the way will have a far better start in life than once seemed possible. During the course of the evening Dave makes a witty speech that has the company laughing and applauding non-stop; and Shirley recalls the time when he used to get tongue-tied trying to show circles at sponsoring meetings. Can that really have been only three years ago?

Of course, all that was a piece of fiction but I have based it as firmly as I can on the growth patterns of actual UK distributorsI have met. And I have included it here as a sort of map to which readers can refer as they read the real life accounts of UK distributors which make up the remainder of the book.

PART II

# ROUND BRITAIN WITH AMWAY

CHAPTER 4

# *Down in the West*

I BEGAN at the end—Land's End. Standing on the much-trampled turf, I gazed westwards, as millions of others had gazed over the centuries, thoughts and feelings surging through me in a confused flood. It cannot be otherwise in this place of rugged beauty so charged with emotional significance for all British people. This massive tumble of granite, pointing into the empty ocean was, indeed, land's end for generations of sailors working out of Bristol, Plymouth or Falmouth in the days of sail. John Cabot was the first pioneer to pass this point bent on proving that there was another continent somewhere beyond the horizon. He planted the English royal standard and a crucifix on the coast of Nova Scotia. A hundred and twenty-three years later the Pilgrim Fathers set out to establish a more permanent Anglo-Saxon presence in North America. In 1901 something intangible sped across the Atlantic from a point not twenty miles from Land's End—Marconi's first long-range radio signal. Yet I was here to examine an impulse which had travelled in the opposite direction. it was a thing called Amway. It had come from America. It had changed the way of life of quite a few people and they believed that it would become a significant force in these islands in the next few years. So I had set myself the task of journeying through England, Scotland, Wales and Northern Ireland to meet some of the people who had got involved with Amway, to see if this American business idea really was working among the conservative British and to assess whether the claims made about its future role here were justified.

*Tea with a philosopher*

I motored in a leisurely way along country lanes, many of them so narrow that it would have been suicidal to travel any faster. I had neither the need nor the desire for haste. The sun was shining and I was not due at my first call till tea time.

I arrived in Falmouth with time to spare. Time to lean on the railings of the little pier and share with a handful of other idlers the undying fascination of boats and water. Scores of small craft dotted the estuary, riding easily at their bright orange mooring buoys. The M/V *St Gerran* loaded a small cargo of trippers, cast off, and puttered seaward *en route* for Helford River,

Rosemullion Head and other beauty spots. I turned and made my way up steeply dipping streets to Veronica Legg's little house.

Veronica is not a local. Like many other residents she was attracted by Cornwall's peace and beauty. She was looking for somewhere quiet to work and for a pleasant atmosphere in which to bring up her two children. She told me all this as she settled me in her sitting room and offered me tea. As we chatted about this and that I gained the impression of a cheerful but thoughtful lady with a ready laugh and a genuine interest in other people. When I asked her more about herself I realised that life for her had been full and varied. Since leaving Cambridge in the 1960s, where she graduated in philosophy and psychology, she had worked as a journalist, been employed on the advice service of the *News of the World*, and spent some time as a psychologist in a medical school in California. She had for some years been a teacher of Transcendental Meditation and was still engaged in this activity. There had been a great deal of fun and excitement in her life but there had been difficulties, too, and she had eventually found herself as the breadwinner for a single-parent family.

It was while she was visiting an old friend in a different part of the country that her host told her about Amway. She responded with academic caution—people with degrees in philosophy and psychology do not easily take to selling soap. On the other hand, well-educated women do not turn down novel ideas just because they are novel. Veronica refused to commit herself. She took away some Amway literature and cassette tapes and studied them very carefully in private. She could find no flaw in either the business plan or the philosophy behind it. On the contrary, all the ideas she met with in Amway and positive-thinking books matched with what she had already learned from meditation—'self-confidence, the fact that things happen when you believe they will happen, the necessity to set yourself goals in life—none of these things were new to me. All the books and tapes did was help me to clarify my thinking.'

Veronica became an Amway distributor because she could see that it would work and that it would produce an ever-growing and secure income, which she certainly needed. She worked steadily and methodically but with an enthusiasm based on total conviction. Within a year she had reached Direct distributor level. I asked if she had ever thought the Amway business *infra dig*. 'Not at all,' she said with a smile. 'Sometimes education can be a block. Clever people may feel they have to do something very prestigious and selling soap is certainly not prestigious. I'm glad about that. It means that Amway is something anyone can do. In my group now there are teachers, hairdressers, travelling salesmen—all sorts of people. I don't think of myself as an academic, anyway, and even if I were it would be of very little use to me in Amway.'

I asked her whether she regarded new friends as the most important single advantage the business had brought her. She weighed the question carefully, 'If I am honest the answer to that has to be "no". I've made far more friends in this last year than I would otherwise have done and I've had a great deal of fun. But right now the really important thing for me is financial security. I think that is something any woman would understand, especially a woman who has to bring up children single-handed. Amway already pays me enough money to live on and I know that it's going to bring in enough for me to have the kind of life I want for the family. That's a possibility I haven't been able to consider since before the children were born. Not only that, there's also the fact that my business doesn't come between me and my family; the children don't have to take a back seat. As far as possible I do most of my Amway work in term time. Then I can spend the holidays with my son and daughter.'

Veronica got up to make another pot of tea and left me browsing along her well-filled bookshelves—poetry, classical literature, theology, devotional works and books by the great thinkers of our own and earlier ages. 'Another thing Amway will do is give me more time for reading and writing,' said Veronica, returning with the tray. 'There are so many things I want to do. It's exciting to know that I will have the time and money to do them.'

We talked of many other things and it was with great reluctance that I eventually had to take my leave. I had enjoyed my tea with a 'philosopher'—a term which I knew would have amused Veronica. There is certainly nothing of the 'blue-stocking' about this vivacious and friendly lady but her education, her spiritual discipline, her studies of the human mind and of great thinkers had equipped her to appraise Amway very critically and one sentence she had spoken stuck firmly in my mind: 'I think I have learned more about philosophy and psychology in this business than I did at Cambridge.'

*They wanted to get off the treadmill*

Forty winding Cornish miles brought me to Wadebridge and the home of Rod and Jill Harrison. Four years ago Rod was a dairy herdsman, living in a tied cottage, putting in more than sixty hours a week for a relatively low agricultural wage. Jill was a nurse—a member of another overworked and and underpaid profession. There were times when several days passed and they hardly saw each other. Like many other young couples they seemed to be trapped in a treadmill existence which had no purpose and which was likely to keep on turning until they reached old age.

It was a relative in Australia who wrote to them about Amway and gave them the address of the English company. They read with interest what he had to say but did nothing about it. Then Jill became pregnant. Now, with the prospect of a loss of income, the Harrisons had to think more seriously about the part-time business offer. They wrote to Milton Keynes and were put in touch with their nearest Direct distributor—who was in Gloucester, a hundred and eighty miles away. They were shown the business. They joined—and became one of the few active Amway distributors in the entire South-west at that time.

It was a situation which would have deterred most people. Not the Harrisons. They were excited at having such a wide field of opportunity. 'After all,' said Rod, 'we could only go forward. As we were we had nothing, so we could lose nothing. We told ourselves we'd just got to do this thing. We said to ourselves "Whatever it takes, we'll do it."' The first year was hard. 'We travelled miles,' Rod explained. 'Wherever there was an Amway meeting or someone who was prepared to listen to the plan, we went.' For months business was static but nothing shook their enthusiasm or determination. In their second year they reached Direct level and, in 1981, they became Ruby Direct distributors.

By that time the real rewards had begun to materialise. They left the tied cottage and bought their own house. Then Rod quit his job. 'It wasn't really planned,' he explained. 'It just happened. My boss was convinced that Amway was insecure; that it wouldn't work. Of course, that just made us more determined. Well, in the spring of 1980 we qualified for Leadership Seminar. We were so excited. I'd never been abroad; never been in an aeroplane; and here we were with a holiday in Spain. There was no way we were going to miss it. I told my boss I should need the first week in October off and he said, "Oh, you can't go then. That's quite out of the question." I said "But I must go." I explained to him that it was a fantastic opportunity. All he said was "Well, you'll have to choose between your job and Amway."' Rod laughed. 'So, I chose.' Rod now does a bit of freelance milking for another local farmer. He works when he wants and only when he wants.

I asked Jill what other benefits Amway had brought them. 'Our daughter now goes to a private nursery school,' she said. 'And we have had some super holidays. We've been to Leadership

Seminar twice and a few weeks ago there was a trip to Ireland at the invitation of our group over there. Perhaps the most important thing is the way it has changed us—especially Rod. His mother says she hardly recognises him. He used to be very quiet and hardly talked to anyone. Now he speaks at rallies and he loves meeting people. In fact, in 1980, we were guest speakers at National Convention.' Rod chimed in enthusiastically 'Oh yes, that really was something else. You can't imagine what it's like to walk out onto that stage in front of thousands of people. The warmth of the welcome you get. It's ... well it's just unbelievable. If the Queen walked out there she couldn't get a warmer welcome.'

'And the future?' I asked. 'Well, I suppose the big thing is hope,' Jill replied thoughtfully. 'We just know that with Amway we can have the lifestyle we want. That includes continuing private education for our daughter, a better house (although we don't hanker after a palace), and I want to make frequent trips to Australia, where most of my family are.' Rod laughed. 'If you wanted to sum up our story,' he declared, 'you'd have to say that our lives have changed all round for the better and they're still changing.'

*Carving a slice out of the cake*

I came by winding ways to ancient Exeter—port, trading post, fortified stronghold, Cathedral city and university town. Today, evidence abounds of its long, eventful history but for most people who throng its streets Exeter is one of the best shopping centres in the west of England. That is one reason why James and Michelle Ryall opened an art gallery there. In fact, the large gallery in a converted warehouse is run by a co-operative; several artists working in various media work and exhibit there.

I was directed upstairs and edged my way past people arranging large canvases of crimson nudes and geometrical blocks of primary colour on the whitewashed walls. In a smaller, first-floor gallery I found a slim young man in tight trousers and a pink shirt working at a long bench, not with paint and canvas but with panels of glass. For James Ryall is a successful craftsman in stained glass. I admired the sketches and designs pinned up around his workshop—abstracts, floral motifs and elaborate patterns—and James told me about the different kinds of work he undertakes, making windows and panels for private homes, churches, colleges, factories, and other buildings.

As we sat on stools and drank coffee brewed on a ring in a corner of the gallery, James told me a bit about his earlier life. 'My father has his own international business and I could have joined him but I didn't fancy sitting behind a desk for the rest of my life just making an awful lot of money. I'm one of those people who likes to set things up for himself. We started this place about ten years ago and it's now one of the best known fine art galleries in the country. I get real satisfaction from deciding to do something worthwhile and building it from the ground floor up. It's been the same with my stained glass; I've established a widespread reputation.'

I asked him if that was his motivation for starting in Amway.

'Well, I do like a challenge,' he said, 'and I had a hankering after something more strictly commerical than my other work. I suppose it was my background coming out. Even so I don't think I would have bothered to go and listen to the plan in the ordinary course of events. But I'd cut my hand on a glazing knife, and some friends invited us to see the business, and Michelle was very keen, so I went. When we saw the plan we liked the look of it and decided to have a crack at Amway. After that we looked very carefully into the business and what we saw really grabbed our imagination.'

'What satisfaction can you, an artist, get out of something purely commercial?' I asked.

'Well, for a start it's nonsense to imagine that because someone is creative he has no interest in making money,' James said firmly. 'I live in a very nice house on Dartmoor and I have a family to support. In my line of work money comes in very irregularly. So the prospect of doing something which would earn a steady income was a strong incentive for starting the business. But, there are lots of other reasons for being in Amway. We've only been in eight months but we could give lots of different answers to the question "What satisfaction do you get out of it?"—money, friends, fun, the products. I suppose in the last analysis it's difficult to define—we just get a buzz out of it.'

I asked James what he thought it takes to be successful in Amway. Do you need to be a good salesman or administrator, for example? He answered quickly and I had the impression that this was a question he had pondered before.

'I think those who are successful in Amway are the sort of folk who would be successful in whatever they did. It's a people business, so you have to get on with people and be sympathetic. You have to have drive and persistence. Of course, Amway often brings these traits out in people who never knew they had them.'

'Is Amway really delivering the goods as far as you are concerned?' I asked.

He nodded enthusiastically.

'Very much so. We haven't made our fortune in eight months;

that would be a bit much to expect but our path is quite clearly charted—Pearl by the end of '82 and Diamond next year. In three years' time I'll be able to retire. I don't suppose I will, but I'll be able to. You see I'm convinced that the only way to "make it" in this country is to go self-employed. And the only self-employed business in which you can be sure of being successful is Amway. I'll always do my stained glass because I enjoy it but it's Amway that's going to make my fortune. It's as though there was a giant cake out there and all we've got to do is go and carve out our slice. We're going to make it. We're putting in five or six evenings a week and it is paying off. There's just no way we're not going to succeed.

We walked downstairs and through the main gallery where the red nudes and panels of rich colour now hung ready for labelling. In a few days potential customers would be scrutinising these works, and some paintings would be finding new homes. James Ryall, I realised was not just an enthusiastic young man. He was an experienced artist and entrepreneur who had proved himself in both spheres and who had earned the right to be taken seriously.

*Infectious enthusiasm*

At Barnstaple they had invited me to a party. 'They' were Lee and Dave Joachim, a young couple living in their own terrace house on the edge of the town. Dave is a manager in the hotel trade. Lee was also involved in hotel work until the arrival of their son last year. 'Our main challenge is time,' said Dave, as he filled my glass with wine. 'I only get two evenings off a week and they can be cancelled at short notice if we get busy in the hotel. That's why we've had to combine events this evening.' He explained that they normally keep business meetings and social evenings separate but that that night they had been 'showing the circles' to some new contacts and afterwards were having a 'pot-luck' for their own distributors. The business meeting had certainly been very lively. Twenty of us, crammed into the front room, saw a presentation of the plan, a product demonstration and heard one or two distributors tell, briefly, why they were in Amway. Then we adjourned to another room for a veritable banquet.

As we jostled, shoulder to shoulder, balancing plates and glasses and endeavouring to make ourselves heard above the hubbub of conversation, I tried to circulate and ask people there what they made of it all. The first man I spoke to turned out to be one of the friends invited along to see the business for the first time. 'Well,' he said, 'they obviously enjoy themselves. I'm not sure I understand why they're all so excited but it's certainly infectious.' Another couple of newcomers entered the conversation. 'Yes,' said a thoughtful middle-aged lady. 'We've decided to join them. We think we'd be silly not to. Opportunities like this don't come along every day, especially when you're not as young as you used to be.'

A smiling, bearded young man eased his way over to us. 'Enjoying yourselves?' he enquired. 'We don't lay on this sort of spread every time just to bribe people into joining Amway, you know.' I realised that this was Iain Williamson, who had MC'd the earlier part of the evening. I asked him what he made of Amway. 'Fantastic people—that about sums it up for me,' he said. 'I've only been in a few weeks, so a short while ago I didn't know any of these folks. Now, some of them are close friends—and I mean close,' he emphasised. 'Let me give you an example. I came down to Lynton a year or so ago to start an antiques business. I didn't know many people in this part of the world. I met a lot through the shop—customers and other dealers. But I could never get really friendly with them because we were almost always in a competition situation; I was trying to buy from them or sell to them. When I came into Amway I found that everyone else wanted to help me, not compete with me. A few weeks ago I had some personal and business problems. I needed someone to look after the shop while I sorted them out. It seemed the most natural thing in the world to turn to my new Amway friends. In fact it was my sponsors who came to the rescue, and they're pretty busy people. Either Amway attracts special people or makes ordinary people special—I haven't quite decided which.' The words bubbled out in an enthusiastic stream. 'I see your glass is empty. If you'd like to make your way over there, Lee will fill it for you.'

I complimented the hostess on a very successful evening. 'We love having parties,' she said. 'And we love telling people about this business. Because of Dave's job we don't manage to get to many rallies and meetings upline. The times that most people are free—Saturdays, bank holidays, and so on—are the very times when the hotel trade is busiest.' 'How on earth do you find time for Amway at all?' I asked. 'I think we all find time for the things that are important to us,' Lee replied. 'We have two free evenings a week and now they're Amway evenings.' 'Why give up all your free time?' I asked. 'Because we want more free time.' Lee paused to replenish a couple of wine glasses. 'We don't want to be stuck with this kind of routine for the rest of our working lives. By giving Amway all we've got for a couple of years we're going to ensure that in the future we can do what we want, when we want, where we want. By the time we go Diamond we shall be able to live at least part of the year in the sun—perhaps in the south of France. That's worth working for, isn't it?'

A little later in the evening I found myself talking to someone else with a great dream. Andy Simmonds works in a chipboard factory. He is a beefy young man with a keen sense of humour. His product demonstration earlier in the evening had been very amusing as well as informative. 'The great passion of my life is martial arts,' he told me. 'The thing I long for above everything else is to get to Japan and study with some of the great masters. Amway is going to make that dream come true.' A far-away look came into his eyes and I knew he could really envisage himself in a totally different culture half a world away. I recalled Joyce Greaves' words 'the British people have forgotten how to dream'. There was no doubt that Amway was helping them recover that faculty.

*Blind faith in Amway*

Terry Day was eighteen when he had the accident. He smashed his motor-bike up and woke in hospital with cuts and bruises but no major damage. He was lucky—or so it seemed at first. Then he began to have difficulty seeing clearly. Rapidly his sight deteriorated. Within a week he was totally blind.

That was twenty years ago. From that day onwards, Terry says, he became a 'second class citizen', a man who would always be pigeon-holed as 'disabled'. 'In many ways that was harder to bear than the actual loss of my sight,' he told me. 'I was always reliant on other people and on charity organisations. They meant well. They helped me a great deal but they always emphasised my limitations. They would say, "We're here to help you. We'll train you for this occupation, or that, but, of course, there are lots of things you'll never be able to do." I rebelled against that attitude. I was determined to prove that there were many things I could do as well as, or even better than, anyone else. I answered "situations vacant" ads and didn't mention the fact that I was blind. It paid off; I got a job. Then, people kept on telling me I was lucky to be employed. So, I still hadn't really escaped from the limitations other people wanted to impose on me. Gradually things improved. I married Pauline, I started my own business. Then Pauline and I took up riding. That was a great help. At last I could get out in the countryside and enjoy real freedom. You don't need a white stick when you're on horseback; just someone to call out when there are obstacles on the path ahead—low branches and that sort of thing. In fact it was through riding that our Amway adventure started.'

I had come to the Day's house in Gosport, Hampshire, because many people had told me that I must be sure to interview Terry and Pauline. It did not take me long to find out why this couple are rapidly becoming well known in Amway circles nor why, after only a year, they have a large and fast-growing group. They are a vivacious, full-of-fun couple. Terry is tall and broad shouldered. He wears dark glasses and an infectious smile. I kept having to remind myself that he was blind because his relaxed conversational style and mischievous sense of humour completely masked any consciousness of his disability. Pauline, is slight, moves gracefully (she teaches movement and dance), and has eye-catching waist-length hair.

She took up the story. 'We went away for a riding holiday and on our last morning there our host and hostess showed us the Amway business. We were immediately excited but we didn't understand it completely. We talked about it all the way home and Terry kept making me stop the car to go over the figures. By the time we got here we had decided that we couldn't afford not to do it. However, we still checked with Companies House to make sure that the business was secure and respectable. We went back a couple of weeks later and joined.'

Terry intervened. 'We joined because the money seemed good but it wasn't long before I realised that Amway was exactly the thing I'd been looking for. Very simply it has taken away my disability. In this business I'm on the same level as anybody else. I'm just as likely to succeed. I've heard so many people make excuses for not getting into Amway and I say to them "If you've got a good reason for not doing it, I've got a better one." You see, there is no excuse, no disability which will genuinely prevent people getting into this business. The only *reason* is you. If you want to do it, you can. Do you know the old poem,

> Everyone told him it couldn't be done,
> But he with a chuckle replied
> Well, maybe it couldn't, but he for one
> Wouldn't say so till he'd tried.

I've spent years proving that true. Over and over again I've done what other people said was impossible. But nothing has given me the same opportunity as Amway. Not only have I been accepted as an equal, I have been able to help other people. I've given them time, advice, encouragement and support and I've seen them develop as people.' He chuckled. 'I suppose it's a case of the blind leading the blind.'

I asked Terry how he managed to demonstrate the business plan to people. He reached into an inside pocket and showed me what looked like an ordinary fountain pen. 'I use my braille pen,' he said. 'It's filled with a special fluid which carries a number of dots. They come out on the paper as I write.' His face was serious. Dark lenses masked his eyes. It was only Pauline's giggle that confirmed my suspicion that I was having my leg pulled. 'He's always doing that to people,' she said. 'He's got a very lively mind and it's a great asset in the business. At our training session last week he was talking about positive and negative mental attitude. He handed round some old photographic negatives of ours and asked people if they could make out what the pictures were. Of course, they could only do it with difficulty. "Yes," he said, "and you can only make sense of life with difficulty if you have a negative mental attitude." I think that's good, don't you?'

Was there anything else Amway had given them apart from a new sense of purpose and personal value? Terry nodded eagerly and launched into a catalogue of benefits 'First it's brought Pauline and I closer together. We now have something to do and plan together. Secondly its extended our social life enormously. Before, most of our friends were in the horse world. Now we have scores of new friends. Most evenings there's a meeting or party somewhere. Thirdly, we've enjoyed recognition and appreciation for all we've achieved. It's great to have genuine acknowledgement instead of being patronised as someone who'd done "jolly well for a blind person". In addition to all that, Amway's given us financial security. My own business has done OK but it's not going to give us all we want out of life because I'm restricted by limited capital and premises, and inadequate staff. We're working towards the point when I can go full time in Amway. We've already decided on the house we want. It's in the New Forest. It's got land and stables. Pauline and I can spend all our time together, riding, and doing other things we enjoy. After that, the sky's the limit.'

I came away from the Days feeling, what, I suspect, most people who meet them must feel: immensely privileged and encouraged.

CHAPTER 5

# *The Heartland*

ROYAL Leamington Spa is the dead centre of England. The estuaries of the Severn, the Dee, the Thames and the Wash—the nearest stretches of tidal water—are almost equidistant. Historically, too, Leamington and its environs can claim a certain centrality. Shakespeare was born and grew up not ten miles away at Stratford. Nearby Warwick Castle was the power base of the Neville and Beauchamp families, whose armies and influence were frequently decisive throughout the Middle Ages. A dozen miles to the south, at Edgehill, the first battle of the Civil War was fought. The Grand Union Canal brought the commerce of the Industrial Revolution right through Leamington at a time when this quiet village was being transformed into a fashionable spa town. A mere four miles up the road lies Kenilworth whose hour of glory came when Elizabeth I's favourite transformed an ancient castle into a sumptuous pleasure house where the queen and her court were entertained with breathtaking splendour and extravagance.

Kenilworth, as we have already seen, is the place where Amway may be said to have begun in Britain. It was from here that the Logans and Nellenbachs started sponsoring new distributors between 1973 and 1977, It was in this pleasant part-rural, part-suburban heartland, ringed by the industrial centres of Birmingham, Coventry, Rugby, Northampton, Oxford, Gloucester and Worcester that the American business put down its roots in English soil. Not surprisingly therefore, this area boasts several strong distributorships.

### *The bulldog spirit*

I had heard Hugh and Lyn Hofton at my first Amway rally in Bristol and again at the 1982 Convention. So I was very much looking forward to meeting them. I knew that they were among the best known and loved leaders in the UK, that they were pioneers who have been in since the beginning and that they had built up a highly successful Diamond organisation.

They live in a seventeenth-century farmhouse on the outskirts of Gloucester and it was there that we talked on a brilliantly sunny day in early summer. Hugh is tall and well-built with a moustache and a ready smile. Lyn, dark, slim, attractive, brought us cold drinks. I drank thankfully after the hot drive and looked around at the wide inglenook fireplace and the old timbers.

'This is me,' said Hugh, tapping one of the beams, 'English through and through.' He spoke with a pleasant Gloucestershire burr. 'I'm just an ordinary English bloke and I love my country. I've got a great admiration for Winston Churchill. We use the bulldog as the symbol of our organisation and we follow Churchill's motto "Never give up". That's how we built our business; sheer, heads-down determination. We weren't going to quit.'

Hugh told me that he had left school at the age of fourteen and drifted in and out of a long succession of jobs, interspersed with periods on the dole. He had become demoralised by repeated redundancies but had eventually been accepted for a government training course and emerged as a plasterer's mate. He then met Geoff Smith and the two of them went into business doing plastering and other building jobs. One day in 1973 Geoff, who had just joined Amway, invited Hugh to a meeting and he and Lyn went along to hear the plan explained by an American couple. Hugh did not take to those loud, brash foreigners but he could not make up his mind whether their business proposition was a con trick or not. Meanwhile Geoff and Jenny Smith were becoming enthusiastic so Hugh and Lyn went along with them to more meetings. Eventually Hugh decided that it was good enough for Lyn to do, so the business was started in her name. But as things got moving Hugh became more convinced and more involved.

Like all the pioneers, Hugh and Lyn had to face the problems of trying to overcome the pyramid selling image and the problem of credibility. How could people believe that real wealth lay in a business which was being hawked by a plasterer's mate who lived in a rented terraced house and drove a scruffy van? That was where the bulldog determination came to their aid. They simply soldiered on. It was incredibly tough. Lyn described it as, 'Showing the circles night after night to women in curlers and carpet slippers who didn't really want to know. There were times when we really despaired of Amway ever working in Britain.' Hugh added, 'The thing that kept me going was fear of the alternative. I had known what it is to be poor and I didn't want to be poor again. Amway was my only chance to get the freedom and the lifestyle I dreamed of.'

Hugh and Lyn confirmed what the Greaves and the Smiths had said about 1976–7 being the turning point. They started developing training programmes, using books and tapes, and things began to come together. Amway started to work the way they had always believed it would work. They found and trained leaders. Steadily, surely, they built up their large, successful organisation. 'One thing I always emphasise—and people really believe it—is that if I can do it they can. You see Amway brings out traits of character and helps you to acquire skills—confidence, persistence, enthusiasm, leadership, ability to speak in public, and so on.'

For the Hoftons perseverance has certainly paid off. They have a lovely home and when they moved they kept on their other property to use as an office. They have complete financial independence. Lyn said, 'We are full time parents to our two-year-old daughter. We have travelled a great deal and before we came into Amway Hugh had never been in an aeroplane.'

I asked them what they saw in the future. Hugh's eyes gleamed. 'The way the business is building we just know some of the great things that are in store. I've always wanted that great symbol of all that's best in Britain—a Rolls-Royce. Well soon I shall have one—probably at the end of this year. Then when we move from here it will be to a Cotswold manor house. It will be really great to have somewhere like that as the centre for our organisation. Lyn added, 'And do you know what will be the nicest thing of all? Being able to fill it with our friends. Rich people have to entertain business associates and people they don't really like. Well, our guests will be great Amway people.'

### *'The last two years were the happiest'*

Apart from providing her with a packed store of happy memories, Michael Grindlay did two important things for his wife before his sad, early death: he built her a lovely house, and he helped her build a thriving Amway business.

As I talked with Liz Grindlay we gazed out of picture windows at the wooded slopes of the Wye valley, dropping steeply to where the river lazily coiled and uncoiled like a silver snake, far below. Every year tourists flock to the famous beauty spot of Symonds Yat but few venture up the steep road where a few 'select' houses and bungalows enjoy the seclusion of their own grounds and the breathtaking view of the valley. Michael, as an experienced builder, knew that he was unlikely ever to find a better site so he decided that he would keep it for himself.

It was because the construction industry was going through a bad patch that the Grindlays decided to say 'yes' when Mike's uncle showed them the Amway plan. At the beginning they did not really understand it. They thought that it was basically a door-to-door operation like other direct-selling companies. It was only when that approach did not work, and they decided to quit, that they discovered what Amway was really about. They took their spare products to Ken and Jane Roberts, their upline Directs, for a refund. The Roberts explained to them more about the business and they decided to have another try. It was a wise decision, for the Grindlays became Direct distributors in six months.

Liz explained that there were two reasons why they put all their available energy into the business: 'The building trade wasn't bringing in enough money. Then, my husband's health began to deteriorate and the urgency seemed even greater'. Michael was certainly a sick man; he was suffering from bone marrow cancer. Nothing the doctors could do was able to arrest the insidious spread of the disease. Michael's activities were gradually restricted until, eventually, he was bedridden. And yet, Liz said, she looked back upon those last two years as the happiest of their married life. She and Michael were working together at something they both believed in and, perhaps, with an intensity that they would not have achieved under normal circumstances. They deliberately went out to meet as many people as possible, in their search for potential recruits. 'We made so many real friends in that short period and that was particularly valuable to me because I had always been a rather shy person.' As Michael grew weaker his dedication to the business did not decline. If anything it became stronger, because he was determined to leave Liz with as large an Amway income as possible.

Michael Grindlay's funeral was a remarkable occasion. Liz found herself supported not only by members of the family but also by more than seventy of her Amway friends. Looking back on that event after two years, Liz said that she did not know how she would have coped without Amway. She was determined to carry on with the business because it had meant so much to her husband. Doing that meant that she was constantly out meeting people and not sitting at home moping. She recalls how the funeral even brought a new distributor into her group. 'There was a cousin we had shown the Amway plan to but he wasn't interested. When he came back to the house here after the service he was absolutely overwhelmed by the sincerity of all our friends. As a result he decided to get into the business.'

I asked Liz if friends were for her, the most important benefits to be gained from Amway. 'Yes,' she said, 'Friends and security. Because I have a strong group with Directs and Emeralds in it I have a good, continuing income. It certainly would not be possible for me to go on living comfortably in this house without Amway.'

I knew, without asking, that it was desperately important to Liz to stay in that lovely house with all its precious associations.

As we drank tea and watched the lower slopes disappear into shadow, I asked her if there was anything else she wanted to tell me. A deep smile radiated her face 'Oh, just make sure your book makes clear that if only people are prepared to put in a lot of effort into starting an Amway business, they'll find the rewards are so very, very much greater.'

### *'We don't need you flash boys here'*

The Green Dragon hotel in Hereford has good reason to be grateful to Amway. Every Sunday morning upwards of a hundred and fifty distributors congregate there for training meetings and scores of other Amway functions have been held there over the past four years. Some of these events have attracted coachloads of people from as far away as Kent and Cornwall. The couple behind all this activity and growth are Emerald Direct distributors Andrew and Sandra Taylor, a lively couple who live with their two young children in an impressive Victorian house on the edge of the town.

The Taylors were sponsored in 1978 by Liz and Michael Grindlay. Incidentally they provide an example of an Amway principle that it is those who do the work who earn the money. When I first began to look at the structure of this organisation it seemed to me that a lot of people at the bottom were making fortunes for a few people at the top. If that were the case the lion's share of profit from the Taylors' huge organisation would be going to Liz Grindlay, who would be very well off indeed. Liz certainly benefits financially for having brought Andrew and Sandra into the business but it is they who have reached Emerald level and who enjoy the income and the advantages that go with it.

The Taylors are business people. Sandra ran an antique shop for a number of years. Andrew, after gaining a Physics degree from Aston University, tried various business ventures before going into partnership in a bakery and restaurant concern. He looks every inch the businessman or senior executive. He dresses well, has a ready smile and an easy manner. He appears totally self-confident. When he is explaining the business he talks rapidly and with enthusiasm. He handles questions deftly and confidently. You feel that, in another context, he would have no difficulty swaying a board of directors or handling an AGM of restless shareholders. His commercial background and training have enabled him to analyse the Amway set-up rationally and develop new techniques of training and communication which have proved strikingly successful. But he readily admitted to me that the 'successful businessman' image can be a disadvantage. A story he enjoys telling is about a visit he paid to a group of distributors in South Wales. He had gone down to the Valleys to take a sponsoring meeting. The evening went, he thought, quite well (and that group has since broken a couple of Directs) and eventually he said goodbye to his host. The little Welshman shook him warmly by the hand and said, 'Thanks for coming Andrew. I reckon we shall be able to manage by ourselves now; we shan't need you flash boys from Hereford here any more'.

He is a perfectionist. For him it is not enough to do something well; he has to do it as well as it can possibly be done. 'For instance,' he told me, 'When I took up golf I felt it was important to win something, so I made it my target to win the knockout championship in the club. I dedicated myself to that task. When I had achieved it, golf became less important; I was able to relax and treat it purely as a hobby. That's how I approach anything I undertake. It was the same with Amway, except that I could see that this business wasn't a question of achieving short-term success and then getting bored with it. It presented Sandra and me with a long-term challenge.' Responding to this challenge meant examining Amway thoroughly, seeing how the more successful distributors worked, travelling to the USA to meet the top people over there and, particularly, trying to devise the best kind of training programme for this country. They came to the conclusion that Amway could be run like a machine. The principles were clear. If you could establish a pattern of operation based on those principles, transmit that pattern to every new distributor, and maintain excellent communication from the top down every line of sponsorship, you would have a smooth-running organisation. Moreover, like a machine, it would be possible to shift the organisation into a higher gear and, therefore, create faster growth. Andrew reckons that Amway was meant to 'fly' and that momentum is an important ingredient in success.

Since their mechanistic system has taken Andrew and Sandra to the Emerald level in three years and since they have a rapidly expanding organisation, their way of doing things obviously works. They have a strong group in and around Hereford and a network of others throughout the length and breadth of the country. They hold quarterly rallies which are regularly attended by hundreds of people, and the consistent numbers attending the weekly training meetings (now duplicated in many other centres) demonstrate the continuing pace of recruitment. Every spring Andrew and Sandra hold a family weekend in Jersey which has become an essential fixture on the Amway calendar for many distributors. For the Taylors themselves, participation in Amway has helped them to acquire a lovely home. Andrew, who loves playing with machines, has been able to buy many 'toys'—a word processor, an electric organ, a multiple cassette tape recorder, to mention but a few. Sandra realised a long-cherished dream when she bought her Mercedes. They have travelled widely in Europe and America, visiting Amway leaders and doing their own international sponsoring. They look back as major influences on their lives time spent with Dan and Bunny Williams and Peter and Eva Muller-Meerkatz. Yet both are agreed that the greatest thing Amway has brought them is 'super friends. We've got more friends, and good friends, from this business than in all our previous lives. With them we have a lot of fun and a full social life. Our nationwide group has a real family feel about it.'

Sandra turned the conversation in another direction. 'It's made an enormous difference to us as a couple,' she said. 'Because of our different educations and backgrounds I used to feel inferior to Andrew. He's got a degree and I was always the dim one, the truant, the class bully. I used to see my role as just supporting Andrew in whatever he did. Amway has given me confidence. I take a full part in the business; I speak at rallies, take meetings and I'm quite happy explaining Amway to really clever people. And what's happened to me has rubbed off on the children. They are growing up into positive, out-going people.'

I asked this dynamic couple how they saw the future. 'Our goal is to be Crown Ambassadors,' said Andrew, without a second's hesitation. And what then, I enquired; would they make their pile and quit? It was meant to be provocative but it drew from Andrew a quiet, well-considered answer. 'We see ourselves as part of an ever-growing group of Diamonds and above all, successful, like-minded people. And we shall all be devoting the greater part of our time and energies to showing other people how to be successful. They may be professionals or businessmen who are tired of the stresses of life. They may be "working class" folk, for want of a better term, who have never had a chance to improve themselves. Whoever they are, we see it as our task to help them realise their dreams.' It was a sentiment I was already becoming familiar with and one I was to hear expressed over and over again during my Amway tour.

### *All for the sake of a new piano*

'Quorn and Thorn', 'Quorn and Thorn'—the words sang repetitively in my head. Quorn because my road lay through the flat fields and past the hedges and ditches of the country regularly hunted by one of England's most ancient packs of fox hounds.

Thorn because I had been told to watch out for the electrical factory on the edge of Fleckney. I saw no pink coats or immaculately groomed horses. I almost did not see the factory. Semi-opaque flurries of rain obliterated the landscape, turning lush pasture and cream stone into a soggy, grey uniformity. But, at last, the name 'Fleckney' stood out clearly against the dull hedgerow and I knew that I was almost at journey's end.

Even through the rain which had subsided to a heavy drizzle I could see that Fleckney combined old and new. Cottages, walled gardens, and ancient church proclaimed that it still clung tenaciously to its village character. Thorn Electric and the accretion of housing for factory workers and Leicester commuters stood for the industrial twentieth century.

Roger and Babs Powdrill, Amway Diamond Direct distributors, live in a detached house overlooking fields on the edge of Fleckney. There are, perhaps, a dozen other similar dwellings on the small development owned, I imagined, by grey suited executives, sitting now at their desks in the city. Some of their wives were probably at work too. But at No 9 the residents were at home and both came to the door to greet me. Everything about the Powdrills' surroundings—the neat garden, the modern furniture, the adventurous decor, the expensive clothes—is tasteful. When they joined Amway, in 1974, they had not long been married. Roger was a qualified pharmacist who had worked for Boots and was then in a smaller shop. Babs, too, was working and it was she who took to the sales and marketing plan at first sight. Roger was unconvinced. Looking back to those days he describes himself as a 'cynical, sceptical, pessimistic, introverted young man'. Retail pharmacy, he explained, is not well paid. It is monotonous and hard work. He had to attract as many customers as possible and cram as many orders as he could into a working day. Experience seemed to tell him that there is no simple or easy way of making money. Financial survival was a matter of solid, daily grind. So when he saw the Amway scheme he said 'That looks marvelous on paper, but I don't believe it will work in practice'. It was only to please Babs that he agreed to take a second look at the business. He was not a hundred per cent convinced even then but he decided to give it a try because he wanted it to be true. 'I thought that it would be nice if it did work,' he said. 'I certainly didn't want to stay in retail pharmacy for the rest of my life and it seemed that Amway just might offer me a way out.'

I asked Babs what she wanted out of Amway in the beginning. She tossed her long blonde hair and laughed. 'A piano!' She gave her husband a look of amused embarrassment. 'Doesn't that sound silly? It's true, though. I love playing and at that time I only had a very battered second-hand piano. In fact it was one of a series of pianos. I used to buy a very old one, play it until it was no more use, then get rid of it and buy another one. So I really longed for a good, new piano that would last.' Roger chipped in 'That's right and there was always the little matter of being able to pay all the bills. We thought that if we could achieve those two simple things our lives would have taken a real turn for the better.'

'And did that happen?' I asked.

'No,' Babs replied. 'Not for eighteen months. We used to sit watching television most nights and telling ourselves the business would work. But we weren't making it work. We saw other people like the Greaves and the Hoftons forging ahead but it took eighteen months for us to decide we were going to put some effort in. We began to have meetings on a regular basis, about twice a week. Then, of course, things started to happen. We went Direct in nine months.'

When I asked Roger what had happened to get their business off the ground after such a slow start he told me that attending rallies and meetings and reading positive thinking books had changed their attitude. When they stopped being shy and introverted and began to believe in themselves they discovered that success was at their feet. Roger gave up his pharmacy work in 1978. They moved house (and, when we met, were planning a further move). They could afford to run two cars and when I met them Roger was looking forward to picking up a new BMW. They had had several holidays abroad. In addition to material rewards they have made very many friends. From being a quiet couple who could number their friends on the fingers of both hands they now have more than they can count. Above all, however, it is freedom that the Powdrills value most. As Babs says, 'It's wonderful to wake up in the morning and say "This is our day. What shall we do with it?"'

Roger and Babs may say that they are much more open and outward-going than they used to be but they are certainly not a wildly extrovert, demonstrative couple. In their own organisation they do not encourage some of the more overt American methods of whipping up enthusiasm at meetings. They are very modest about their own achievements in Amway and the thousands of people who, directly or indirectly, owe their start in the business to the quiet couple from Fleckney. As to their future, Roger told me that they had no burning desire for a millionaire lifestyle. For the moment, at least, they are looking no further than the Double Diamond level and the £50–60,000 a year that goes with it. Yet he was quite convinced that they would go on working the business, resetting their goals as they passed the milestones of success.

I asked Roger if, looking back over the last seven years he could identify one quality necessary for success in Amway. He did not have to think about his reply. 'Sheer guts,' he said. 'If you just stick at it and overcome all the obstacles you meet you will become a much stronger person and you'll enjoy life much more because you *are* a better and stronger person. We will always be grateful to Amway for providing us with a lot of challenges.'

I had a striking example of the need for endurance later that day. The Powdrills arranged for me to call on Pete and Val Henton. So, a dark wet night found me knocking at the door of a terraced house in Leicester. It was very different to the Powdrills' village residence. Here was no thoughtfully-decorated home—an extension of the occupants' personalities. It was, I felt, simply a building in which the Hentons happened to live. The 'SOLD' notice outside proved the point.

Pete and Val regard their Amway story as a cautionary tale. When they started their business in 1974 they really needed success. Pete went through a number of jobs—electrician, milk roundsman, service engineer. They had two very small children. And they were poor. Peter still vividly remembers pouring out his troubles to a stranger in a pub who gave him five pounds to buy a puppy for his daughter. Yet for all that they failed in Amway. They worked at the business sporadically. They reached the 21% level, then dropped back again. Why? They put it down to low general morale and Pete's stubborn determination to do things his own way. Like many men he had started off convinced that Amway was 'a little selling business for the wife'. It was not the sort of thing that a self-respecting head of the household got involved with. When he did, at length, take an interest he still treated Amway as a conventional retail business. He gathered a few distributors and provided them with products to sell. He had no intention of helping other people to build businesses that might compete with his own.

The Hentons occasionally went to rallies and meetings; they even met Rich de Vos. But it took almost five years for them to make a fresh and decisive start. The reason was that before anything else could happen Pete had to admit that he was wrong. He had to be prepared to learn from the people upline whose lifestyles were obviously changing for the better and realise that the only method worth using was the one being used by the successful.

In mid-1979 they made the important decision. Within a year they had built a stable Direct distributionship. They were earning a substantial second income. They were beginning to enjoy luxury holidays and Amway seminars. They felt for the first time that they had status, a status which would lift Pete out of his dull job, which would convey them to a better house and which would entail private education for the children. Much of Pete and Val's thinking centres on their little boy and girl. 'We want them to be exposed to the sort of positive people this business attracts,' Val said. 'It isn't just being at the top that's important; it's the people you're with. Amway people are going to make up much of the environment our children grow up in. We couldn't ask for anything better.'

As I said 'goodnight' and stepped out into the rain-spattered street the 'SOLD' notice rattled in the wind. I realised it was not just a house that the Hentons were changing.

### *Send in the clones*

A couple of years back the issue of genetic engineering was a topic of popular controversy. It was brought to the fore by the claims of an American scientist that he could, by chemical processes, predetermine the characteristics inherent in a human foetus—in other words that he could 'create' certain kinds of people. Whatever the superficial attractions of a world populated by men and women 'programmed' to be non-aggressive, gentle and understanding, most of us would, I think, prefer to preserve individuality. We want to be free, even if it means being free to be unreasonable, bad-tempered and downright beastly. So we are suspicious of anything that seems to produce stereotyped attitudes and duplicate personalities. This is the sort of charge that has been levelled against Amway by some critics. One newspaper article unequivocally stated, 'Amway works on clone principles ... the would-be distributors compile a list of acquaintances then invite them to an informal presentation at home ... more important than selling soap, they want to sell the idea of becoming clones, joining in the Amway business for themselves ...'* Others have pointed to the use of certain kinds of books and cassette tapes as evidence of 'brainwashing'.

These suggestions ran through my mind as I ate a leisurely breakfast in the Post House at Leicester. I suppose it was the Hentons' insistence that they wanted their children to be influ-

* Lynn Faulds-Wood in *Daily Mail*, 29 January 1980.

enced by Amway people that had set me thinking along these lines. Is there such a thing, I wondered, as an 'Amway person'? I certainly seemed to have encountered many common attitudes and thought patterns among the distributors I had met so far. With some difficulty, I jotted them down in biro on a paper napkin. After about five minutes I had an interesting list:

Optimism
Belief in free enterprise
Belief in self-help
Self-confidence
Ambition
Tenacity
Enthusiasm
Desire to help others
Hunger for success

I scanned the ten qualities. Did they apply to all the Amway people I had met? Yes, in varying degrees, they did. Certainly they were the hallmarks of all those people at higher levels in the business whom I had interviewed. I recalled the Powdrills and others who had insisted how much Amway had changed their attitudes and personalities. Was there anything sinister about this, anything that would merit the taunt of 'cloning'?

A snatch of conversation reached me from a neighbouring table.

'It's all very well for old Peters to say everything's got to be properly processed. He doesn't have to face the customers.'

A disgruntled company rep was talking with a colleague.

'Anyway I tell them now "If you've got any delivery complaints get straight onto me and I'll deal with them".'

'That's not your job,' his older companion pointed out.

'It's either that or lose orders, isn't it? Something's got to be done about Despatch. I'm going to bring it up at the monthly meeting.'

I seemed to have heard an almost identical conversation in another hotel only a few days before. I looked at the two men. They wore conservative, off-the-peg grey suits and quiet ties. One of them was already on his third cigarette. Glancing round the dining room, with its decor based on the heyday of English canal transport, I saw that there were a dozen similar businessmen fuelling themselves with sausage, egg, bacon and fried bread, in readiness for the rigours of the day. They were uniformly dressed. Shortly they would be leaving the hotel with their regulation brief cases and climbing into their company Cortinas. They had had similar training. Their success or failure as salesmen would depend on the degree to which they had absorbed certain techniques and attitudes.

Were they clones? Surely not—any more than the waitresses with their tidy yellow and brown dresses. Every job requires certain characteristics. Those who do not possess or develop those characteristics usually quit and look for something else. Very few of us are square pegs who are lucky enough to find holes of exactly the right size and shape to fit into. Most of us require a bit of carpentry. Salesman, waitress, missionary, doctor, mechanic, Amway distributor—all willingly undergo training and self-adaptation to fit them for their chosen role. I suppose there will always be an unhappy minority of misfits who isolate themselves by an inner conviction that they are incapable of change and that society must adapt to meet their needs. From their ranks come our political agitators, religious fanatics, criminals and geniuses. There will certainly always be a larger group of people who allow themselves to be moulded by circumstances and the, often-contradictory, pressures life applies to them. The wiser course, it seems to me, is that followed by those who decide what sort of people they want to be, what sort of life they want to live, what kind of job they want to do, and who set about programming themselves for a planned future. Was it not this sort of 'brainwashing' St Paul had in mind when he wrote, 'fill your minds with everything that is true, noble, good and pure, everything we love and honour, everything that can be thought virtuous or worthy of praise'?

Amway people have made a deliberate decision to train themselves to think and behave in certain ways. There is no loss of individuality about that. They have taken a course of action which involves acquiring certain attitudes and jettisoning others; devoting their time to some activities and sacrificing others; making new friendships and giving up old ones. They have set themselves to overcome all obstacles to gain a state of life in which they believe they will be better, happier and richer. They have weighed up the pros and cons of Amway and they have made their choice. A clone has no choice.

### *The company viewpoint*

I headed south for my next port of call. This was to be something quite different from meeting distributors in their own homes. I was going to Milton Keynes to see the headquarters of Amway (UK) Ltd and to meet the General Manager, Stewart McArthur. In fact this meant visiting two separate sites—the premises at Stony Stratford which had housed the growing business since 1979, and the new complex beside the M1 at Tongwell which was then nearing completion. (It was opened on 20 September 1982.)

Stewart McArthur is a tall, dark, handsome, no-nonsense, canny Scot. He had considered very carefully whether or not he would help with my book. He is obviously the sort of man who makes decisions cautiously and sticks to them firmly. Once he had made up his mind about my project there was no wavering: he was generous with his time and gave me all the information I required. He has been with Amway (UK) Ltd, since 1976, longer than most of the 180 other employees in the offices and warehouse. As we toured the premises it soon became obvious that a distinctly American style of staff relations prevailed. The General Manager is 'Stewart' to the girl at the typewriter and the man on the loading bay. He exchanged some banter with 'Tom', who was checking orders, about the previous Saturday's football match, in which both had played. He explained how the team would shortly be travelling to the continent to play against Amway (France) Ltd.

'Keeping the staff happy is vitally important in an operation like Amway,' he said. 'So many of our people are in direct contact with distributors. They have to understand how the business works and that means a fairly extensive training programme for each new employee. We have a very active sports and social club. Every month I have a 'speak-up' meeting when staff representatives put their points of view very frankly and we thrash out any grievances. We pride ourselves on the package of remuneration and conditions we offer our people. For example, Tom and the others in the checking department are on a team bonus system for volume and accuracy. That means they keep each other up to the mark. That's why we have a current error rate on orders of only 1.5 per cent. That's not bad when you consider that every order is unique and is made up by hand from over 220 different stock-keeping units. Then again, business is expanding so rapidly that we have had to increase staff from 50 to 180 in the last year.' I remarked that 180 seemed rather a small number of employees to be managing a nationwide organisation.

'That's because, being comparatively new, we are able to use the latest technology. We have an IBM System 38 computer to control our stock flow and distributor bonuses.' He pointed out the consoles that a row of clerks were using to process orders. 'We have an even bigger computer being installed at Tongwell. Business growth is running at 160% per annum. So, to keep a good staff/work ratio we have to increase staff and technology in the right proportions. We plan for a total workforce of about 400 in three years' time. We reckon that will be enough to cope with continued expansion till the end of the decade.'

I asked Stewart how he and his staff felt about seeing their distributors become wealthy while they remained on fixed salaries, since Amway employees may not be distributors.

'We certainly have a challenge there,' Stewart agreed. 'We pride ourselves on providing the staff with a good opportunity internally. Then, we try to ensure that the philosophy expounded by the founders and used by the distributor organisation also operates within the buildings. In our training we emphasise that the distributors' success is our success. But if, at the end of the day, someone in the Company decided that he could have a greater future as a distributor we would applaud his enterprise and wish him the best of luck.'

We toured the four buildings from which the entire Amway operation was controlled. 'It's an operational nightmare,' Stewart admitted. Everyone's going to be so glad when we get into the new location. I saw the offices where girls sat processing the thousands of orders that arrive in a continuous stream. Nearby, other desks were piled with distributor bonus accounts. In a neighbouring section thousands of applications from new distributors were being handled every month. On to the warehouse with its towering racks crammed with cartons bearing names by now becoming familiar—L.O.C., See Spray, Dish Drops, SA8.

'As you can see,' Stewart waved a hand around the capacious but well-filled interior, 'we're at capacity. We can't wait to get into our new warehouse. I am constantly amazed by the people here who fill all the orders without delay. When you think that we service all the distributors from Land's End to John o' Groats from this building, every week—well it's little short of amazing.' From the warehouse we crossed to another block where all the administration was handled, including the production of Amagram, and the planning of conventions, leadership seminars, Diamond forums and Direct distributor seminars.

We climbed into Stewart's car for the short drive to Tongwell. As we passed through the unimaginative, still incomplete, industrial complex—angular buildings scattered over the landscape like discarded toys—we talked about the growth of Amway (UK) Ltd. The General Manager pointed out the rows of custard-coloured boxes that constitute part of the Kiln Farm estate. 'We started in 1973 in one of those horrendous yellow buildings,' he said. 'Our present accommodation was opened by Rich de Vos in September 1979 but, by then, plans were already afoot for the Tongwell development.' What eventually emerged from those early planning sessions was the purchase of a 5.6 acre prime site and the building of a 100,000 square foot complex with further expansion capabilities. I asked what it was all going to cost. The answer was prompt 'Four million pounds'. He paused while he swung the car onto the Newport Pagnell road. 'I guess there aren't many companies experiencing the expansion necessary to justify that kind of commitment, at the moment.' There was another gap in the conversation while the car waited to pull out and pass a long-load vehicle. 'Then you have to realise that the incredible sales growth we're getting is all down to the distributor organisation. There's no way we can drum up extra turnover. It's just individuals and groups who see the Amway opportunity and use it to improve their lot.'

It was clear to me, now, that the confidence felt by most distributors was more than matched on the Company side. But could this faith in continued growth really be justified. 'Surely,' I asked, 'it's difficult to plan so far ahead?'

Stewart smiled. 'It may sound like a typical management press-release,' he said, 'but we believe we have some of the most sophisticated techniques of forecasting available both in this country and in America. Also, we can draw on the experience of Amway operations all over the world. We take into consideration sales figures, applications from new distributors, population density, expansion of product range and other factors. Our projections may look pretty hair-raising to the layman but we are confident that they are accurate. Amway UK's market potential is £3–400,000,000 per annum. We haven't scratched the surface of that yet. But we look like being the biggest marketing organisation in the country by the end of the decade. You see, there is literally no limit to the size of the product range. We have currently over 200 stock-keeping units. In the USA that figure is in excess of 3,000 and, in any one month, they are testing around 300 new ideas. Only a few of those ideas reach the market because Amway are committed to providing distributors with unique products of a high standard.'

'But, being practical,' I persisted, 'There must be some areas Amway will never move into—food for instance.'

'Derek, nothing would surprise me with this organisation. We're already into health foods and we have a pattern of continuous product-range expansion. Who would have thought twenty years ago that we would have fire alarms and smoke detectors? No, when you look to the future the mind boggles.'

We pulled up in front of the two new buildings and I had my first look at the development which represented a four million pound commitment by Amway Corporation to their British distributors. I had to imagine the mud replaced by a tidy parking area, lawns and shrubs but the office and warehouse blocks were externally complete. They were spacious, functional but attractive, constructions of dark-red brick and tinted glass. We were taken round by the site manager. It was clear from the conversation that a healthy respect existed between Amway and the contractors, Kyle Stewart Ltd. The work had been scheduled to take just over a year and, despite one of the wettest and coldest winters on record, only five weeks had been lost. Therefore, even where the internal fittings were not complete it was easy to imagine the finished effect. We saw the reception area, with its floor of polished stone and the boards where all Direct distributors' names would be displayed. We toured the sound-proofed managerial offices and the canteen where all staff, from General Manager to van driver will eat together, the conference room with its hessian-finished walls and adjacent film projection room, the open plan general offices and the computer room—already increased in size since the plans were first drawn up. The warehouse was in itself a dramatic illustration of Amway's current and future expansion. With a floor area of 60,000 square feet it was considerably larger than the building it was replacing and it was to be equipped with the latest mechanised sorting and packing system. I could not help but be impressed. Yet as I scribbled notes, Stewart McArthur and the Kyle Stewart man were already talking about 'phase one expansion' in 1983–4. I thought of the converted petrol station in Ada where all this had begun. It seemed that De Vos and Van Andel had the Midas touch—wherever in the world they started a new operation their pattern of astounding and persistent growth was repeated.

We returned to Stony Stratford and a sandwich lunch in Stewart's office. A problem had cropped up in Dublin which was going to require the General Manager's presence that afternoon, so we had to forgo a more leisurely meal. I asked him whether he foresaw Amway becoming a challenge to such industrial giants as Unilever and Procter and Gamble, who obviously had the commercial muscle to squeeze out unwanted competition. He shook his head.

'In the States Amway have about 1.8% of the potential market and that's after twenty-three years. Over here our market share is small. Because of our movement into new product fields all the time I don't believe we will be seen by major manufacturers as dangerous competitors in this century.'

Suddenly I saw the whole Amway operation clearly. It was as though, up till that moment, I had been stumbling around a darkened room, making out the shapes of tables, chairs and cupboards piecemeal. Now the light had been switched on and the arrangement of the furniture was immediately obvious. The ever-increasing product range was the key to Amway's commercial success. Not only did it avoid potentially costly competition with major manufacturers, it gave security to company and distributor organisation alike. Amway's eggs were in a multitude of baskets. Sluggishness in one market area would always be counterbalanced by expanding sales elsewhere. Acclimatising new customers to standards of excellence such as they were not used to finding in the supermarket disposed them towards buying other Amway products, until ultimately they would do virtually all their shopping through their Amway distributor. For the distributor himself the constantly-expanding range meant that there was no limit to his potential earnings. His was not just a soap business. The dynamic provided by this limitless expansion was, to use Stewart McArthur's words, 'mind-blowing'.

It was quite clear that the General Manager was totally committed to Amway and that he enjoyed his work immensely. When I asked him how he saw his business future he told me that although other opportunities had crossed his path, Amway offered something that could not be replaced. 'I get an enormous kick out of seeing ordinary people improve their lot by grasping the Amway opportunity. At this moment in time, I can't see myself doing anything else.'

We shook hands. As I prepared to take my leave and Stewart adjusted his thoughts to the Irish question, I had a long last look at this honest Scot. Was he a Company mouthpiece or did he really mean what he said? There was no doubt in my mind about the answer to that question.

CHAPTER 6

# *Land of my Fathers*

LLANTWIT MAJOR is a small town of narrow, twisting streets and picturesque houses. At least, I think the houses were picturesque. The trouble was I was concentrating so hard on negotiating the narrow streets that I could not really look at them very carefully.

The house where Peter and Stella Davies live, however, is certainly attractive and they were kind enough to take me on a tour of it. It is a tall Victorian building with spacious rooms which the owners have decorated in excellent taste. Peter and Stella are Ruby distributors and leading figures in the growth of Amway in South Wales. Peter, a tall, youthful man, runs a very successful group of estate agency offices and is a well known local figure. Stella started her Amway business in 1978, before she met Peter, and had established a highly successful Direct distributorship by the time they fell in love. Peter had seen something of Amway in the USA—and not been very impressed—but when he really studied the sales and marketing plan he became very enthusiastic.

Amway has paid handsome dividends. The certainty of an increasing income enabled them to buy and renovate their lovely home. It has paid for expensive holidays, including a trip to Ada and other places in the USA. But Stella, a very attractive, poised young lady, told me that for her money was not the most important thing. 'Amway has given me confidence. I used to be terribly shy. When I started in Amway, my foster sponsor, Ken Roberts, had to take my meetings for a year. I used to be nervous even asking people if they wanted coffee. My business certainly started slowly. It was nine months before I sponsored someone who stayed in.' 'Stella certainly has stickability,' Peter commented, 'and that's something we stress at our training meetings.'

He told me that as a businessman he had come to have the highest respect for the Amway operation. 'It's not just the high ethics, the professionalism and the brilliance of the sales and marketing plan; it's the human element. Representatives of this organisation, from the top down, really care about people. We've been to Ada. We know the spirit that pervades that place. But the best personal proof we have is that we wrote to Rich De Vos last year to ask him for a message we could relay to a big meeting we were planning. He actually took the trouble to record a tape for us so that he could speak personally to our group. There can't be many leaders of international corporations who would do that.'

Peter and Stella have an excellent lifestyle. They enjoy a professional image, a lovely home and social acceptability. The estate agency is booming and Stella has a very well paid job with British Telecom which she really enjoys and would be foolish, at the moment, to give up. Although Amway has given them important extras did they really need a part-time business, I asked.

'Well, for one thing,' Stella replied, 'I love it so much I'd find it hard to give it up. For another its very good to have a business which is so reliable. If times are hard the house market may slump but Amway just keeps on growing. So if ever we need more income all we have to do is work a bit harder at Amway. But, I suppose the real reason is freedom. We're taking this business to Diamond and beyond. When we've done that neither of us will need to work at anything else if we don't want to.' Peter confirmed that. 'The time may come when I'll put a manager into the agency,' he said. He added 'I think it's very important that there are people like us in Amway. Colleagues I meet in professional circles look at Stella and me and say, "Well, they're obviously not in Amway because they need the money. Perhaps there really is something in this thing."'

*Amway in the Valleys*

The traveller cannot help but be aware that Wales is a different country. The signposts are in two languages. The village names are unpronounceable. In shops and streets people talk to each other in a tongue which is a joy to listen to but is impossible to understand. The Welsh are a people apart. Yet, as I learned from the Davies and other distributors, Amway has been received just as enthusiastically here as in England. There is a particularly flourishing organisation in the Cardiff area and another growing in Swansea.

But I was leaving these places behind me, heading up into the mountains towards the traditional heavy industrial heart of Wales, an area steeped in popular mythology, an area of slag heaps, deep shaft mines, tiny industrial communities, roaring iron foundries and male voice choirs—the Valleys.

'There was a time when you couldn't see down there for thick red smoke. Much as I like fresh air I would love to have that time back.'

It was Edith Bracey who spoke those wistful words as we stood outside her terraced cottage on the steep hillside and looked down on the silent steel works of Ebbw Vale. The railway sidings were empty, the chimneys devoid of smoke, no industrial din challenged the supremacy of birdsong. Where the outsider saw peace, the people of this community were only aware of desolation, and thousands of lost jobs.

A few minutes later we were sitting in Edith's lounge with her husband, Walter, and downline distributor, Anne Rhead. 'We are very thankful we got into Amway when we did,' Walter explained. 'That was 1980. We were both in the steel works but it was collapsing all around us. At the time we only saw it as a means of making some pocket money. It was some while before we saw the possibility of a substantial income but, by golly, we value it now. So many of our friends have lost their jobs, their income and their self-respect. But we have an income and we've also made a lot of friends.'

'People in the Valleys are very conservative and cautious,' Edith said. Anne agreed. She told me how she and her husband, Cyril, had come to join. 'We were invited by some friends, Peter and Iris, to go to a business meeting. We didn't know what it was about but we went along for a giggle. And there was this very excited girl, Sandra Taylor, showing the plan and we got quite interested. But when I discussed it with Iris afterwards she said, "Oh, I don't know about it. Peter's keen but I'm not sure. I think we'll wait and see what you decide." Now, she had seen the plan before and she had introduced us. Yet she was waiting for *our* reaction before she made up her mind. Well, fortunately, we decided to do it and we worked hard and built up a group of about 140 distributors. Peter and Iris came with us and now they're keen as mustard. But, you see, that's what life is like in these close communities.'

I sensed a frustration in what they were saying. They were talking about people they loved, people they had grown up with, people whose roots, like theirs, were in these, once flourishing Valleys. They had no desire to be anywhere else and they wanted to bring the obvious benefits of Amway to their neighbours. They desperately wanted success for those neighbours, many of whom were suffering as a result of the recession in the steel industry.

'As time goes by, more and more of them will see it,' Walter said. 'We just have to lead by example. When we go Diamond and have many of the good things of life, they'll realise that they can travel the same road. We love helping people (for eleven years the Braceys did voluntary work in a psychiatric hospital) and we are going to help more and more people here rebuild their lives. Lots of us are doing it already but there's plenty of room for more people in Amway.'

CHAPTER 7

# *The North-West Explosion*

I JOURNEYED north, over the Brecon Beacons and the hills of Powys to the valley of the young Severn where it rushes into Newtown, then slows to a more sedate pace to amble through Welshpool. On through Oswestry and Wrexham with its marvellously exuberant church tower. And so to half-timbered Chester, opulent and secure within its ancient walls.

Gerald Tilson is one of the city's better known inhabitants. As an auctioneer and estate agent of many years' standing he could hardly be otherwise. But he and his wife Cynthia are also involved in many local activities such as the organising of the Cheshire County Show, and membership of the county council. Gerald's first love is antique furniture and he is never happier than when he is valuing oak dressers, mahogany bureaux, and bracket clocks, or surrounded by objects of beauty and craftsmanship in his busy saleroom. He and Cynthia have a number of fine pieces of their own and three years ago they found the ideal setting for them—a large eighteenth-century sandstone village house. It was derelict and most of their energies have gone into turning it into a beautiful home, combining grace and comfort.

We sat in the kitchen of Hollybank so as not to disturb a young daughter at her piano practice and I asked why an evidently successful professional man and public figure should make time in his life for Amway. The answer was well weighed and carefully delivered. 'We see this business as providing financial independence. I enjoy auctioneering but I would like to withdraw from it, partially at least, to become a consultant. Then I could spend more time at home with the family and doing other things that interest me.'

The Tilstons had been in Amway almost a year and had reached the 21% level. I asked them what they made of it. 'It's very exciting,' Cynthia said and Gerald added, 'I get as much thrill out of showing the plan as I do knocking a painting down for £36,000. It's exciting, it's fun and it's all to do with people.'

They told me how they had seen the potential of Amway as soon as they were shown the plan. This was something I had noticed with other business people I had come across; they seemed to be able to grasp quickly what Amway is about and make a response one way or the other. Being such a public figure, did Gerald not have some hesitation about involving himself in an unknown business, I asked. 'Not at all,' he replied. 'We're always open to new ideas and we could see that this was right. We're delighted we were shown the Amway opportunity. Quite apart from the money, it's given us a lot of fun. Like the disastrous product demonstration I did at one of my early meetings. It was for a new distributor who lived alone with his mother. He was not the most organised of men. First of all I asked for black shoe polish so that I could show how LOC cleans stubborn grease off hands and material. He hadn't got any. He could only offer clear furniture polish, which hardly provides a dramatic demonstration. However, I had to make do. When I had put the polish on my hand and rubbed in the LOC I asked him for a clean white hanky. He hadn't got one. I sent him to find the next best thing. He returned with a grubby white shirt. The audience by this time was suffering from muffled hysterics. They had seen nothing yet! Having wiped the mess off my hand I then had to try to get the shirt into a small bowl of water to show how easily the strain is removed. This proved both impossible and messy. I decided to pass rapidly on to the Drain Mate demonstration. You put the blue liquid into a glass of water then dissolve polystyrene chips in it to show how it dissolves fats and grease in drains and wastepipes. My host had provided me with a narrow specimen glass into which I could not get my fingers to push down the polystyrene. Nothing daunted, I used a cheap felt-tipped pen to do the job. The polystyrene dissolved most impressively—so did the pen!'

I did not have to go too far for my next call. Chris Quartermaine is also a Chester businessman. He has a chain of health food shops. Like the Tilstons, Chris and Katie also said 'yes' to Amway as soon as they saw it. Their experience in commerce had conditioned them to look for something simpler, more reliable and less capital intensive. Chris, a slim, bearded young vegetarian, told me some of the problems of being a shopkeeper. 'Running a conventional business eats more money than it gives. I have a very successful shop in Chester. That is profitable just as long as someone else doesn't come along and set up in competition. So the only way I could secure a growing income was by opening more shops. So I started two more in other towns. I rented one in Macclesfield only to discover, too late, that it had dry rot which cost £3,500 to put right. So what with that, and staff problems and inflation I've learned the hard way that you can only grow by borrowing more and more money. You can end up mortgaging your life away to make your business grow. When Amway came along we saw that here was a business which didn't require capital, in which we didn't have to employ anybody, which would grow by our own efforts, and which would give us the certainty of a continuing income.'

'What I like about Amway,' Katie added, 'is that it's a business we can work together. I get continually frustrated with the shops because it's very difficult for me to be involved.'

So, I asked, would they be giving up the shops.

'Yes, I've reduced my commitment to four days a week and we plan to sell the shops in a couple of years,' said Chris. 'And then,' Katie added, 'it will be Amway all the way.' She laughed, then was suddenly serious. 'Some people in the group know what their big dreams are—one wants to run a craft centre, and so on. I haven't found my big dream yet but I know it's there. When I've got the money I'll know what I have to do with it.'

*Lighting the Fuse*

As you sit nose-to-tail on the motorway in a queue of vehicles that shuffles slowly above the roofs and factory chimneys of Greater Manchester, you certainly have time to think. Indeed that is probably the only way of maintaining a semblance of calm and sanity. The thought that thrust itself into my mind as I gazed at the rimless ocean of brick and slate was that slogan 'Made in England', once the most prestigious label any manufactured item could bear. For almost two hundred years this expanding city had proudly pumped its wares into the commercial arteries of the Empire and the world—cotton garments, printed calicos, machine parts, electronic components, canned foods and the first plastic goods. And now? Many of its mills and workshops are silent. A growing number of its citizens are on the dole. And the wares which so often outclass home-produced manufacturers in terms of quality and price bear the names of foreign countries of origin—Japan, Taiwan, Hong Kong, the Federal German Republic, Czechoslovakia.

Is this turn round to be explained purely in economic terms—the changing pattern of world trade and the loss of our colonies? Or is there a deeper, spiritual malaise underlying Britain's commercial and industrial decline? When Manchester was no more than a thriving market town, the poet John Milton addressed an angry pamphlet to the leaders of the nation. It began in this stirring vein:

> 'Lords and Commons of England! consider what nation it is whereof ye are, and whereof ye are the governors; a nation not slow and dull,

> but of a quick, ingenious and piercing spirit; acute to invent, subtle and sinewy to discourse, not beneath the reach of any point the highest that human capacity can soar to.'

Within a few decades of those words being written, this great city had begun its growth—a very tangible testimony to the truth of the blind poet's words. It was imaginative invention, entrepreneurial skill and conscientious industry that gave this tiny island its commercial mastery throughout the world. So what has changed? Has native ingenuity now dried at the source? Have skills been unlearned? Has the willingness to work hard been sapped by lack of incentive? I for one would be very reluctant to accept any of those alternatives. There is, it seems to me, a deeper cause for our malaise; it is a failure of belief. No amount of social engineering or political activity can motivate a nation or an individual who no longer has faith in his ability to achieve great things.

I was on my way to meet some people who certainly had faith and had achieved great things. In the late seventies there was a real upsurge of Amway activity in the North-west. It was the first dramatic example of regional growth and it has gone down in the annals as the 'North-west Explosion'. The couple who lit the fuse were Robert and Suzanne Hayward. They live in a detached, Georgian style house in a pleasant suburb of Stockport. Since they joined Amway in 1974 they have become Emerald Direct distributors and Robert has given up his job as a computer systems designer. We settled in deep, modern armchairs in the Haywards tastefully-decorated lounge and Robert, a slim, moustached man in his thirties explained that Suzanne was unfortunately out for the evening.

He explained that when they first saw the plan they were a shy couple who had been married only six months. He immediately saw in the 'circles' a means of paying the mortgage but Suzanne rejected the Amway concept completely. Robert explained, 'She was an occupational therapist. She had a professional image to maintain. The last thing she wanted was to go door-to-door selling, which was what she thought Amway was. However, we decided to have a go and when Suzanne actually tried the products then she, too, got switched on. We started working the business in January 1975 and, in the first month, we sponsored five couples. We thought it was easy. But we knew little about the business. Our sponsor, Rob's brother George, lived 150 miles away and in those early days there was very little in the way of knowledge or training. Consequently, by March we found ourselves on our own again. Not surprisingly, our enthusiasm waned. For eighteen months, until September 1976, we did virtually nothing with the business. But we did go pretty regularly to Amway functions, especially rallies organised by Hugh and Lyn Hofton in Gloucester, and what we found there was real friendship. We got to know Hugh and Lyn well and several other distributors and we were brought out of our shells—especially Suzanne.'

It was the annual convention in September 1976 that really started the ball rolling for the Haywards, as Robert told me. 'The hall seemed to be full of successful people and we felt out of place. We sat at the back. At lunchtime we ate our sandwiches in the car because we didn't want to talk to anyone. We even sat in different seats when we came back because we didn't want to be recognised. It was as we were leaving at the end of the day that Lyn came up to us and said, "This time next year you could be standing on the convention stage as the newest Direct distributors in the UK." We went home and made the all-important decision to take the business seriously. But we reckoned that people in the North-west were different; they would never take to Amway. So we seriously considered moving job and house to Gloucester because we thought that was where it was at.

'A few weeks later Hugh came up to take a meeting in Manchester and he stayed with us for a couple of nights. On both nights he and I sat up talking till well into the morning. That wore me out but I noticed that, whereas I had to get up to go to work, Hugh didn't. He had already put in the time and gained the success that had given him freedom. Hugh told us that Amway would work just as well in the North-west as anywhere else and that we could either pioneer the growth here or watch someone else do it.' From that point on the Haywards' business grew steadily. By the time of the next convention they were, indeed, Direct distributors. 'That taught us the importance of setting goals,' Robert said. 'We wrote on the ceiling above our bed the date we were going Direct. Ever since then we have set ourselves various goals and charted a career path to success. We really set out to learn all we could about the business. We went to America for a month and attended various meetings including a west coast convention, where there were 14,000 people, and we visited Ada.'

Then I asked Robert how the 'North-west Explosion' had originated. 'It began in February, 1979,' he said. 'We got together with a number of other very keen distributors, and we realised that what was missing in our group was a sense of unity. So, the first thing we decided to do was give ourselves a name and we fixed on the "North-west Explosion". From that point people really began to feel part of a team. We took every possible opportunity of telling them all how proud we were of them. We told them they were "the best", not out of a sense of competition with other groups, but just so that they would know how highly we regarded them. And the more we told them that the more they lived up to it. We had our first Direct distributors by September and then the flood gates really opened and lots of people began to reach Direct level. By 1982 there were scores of distributors at Ruby, Pearl and Emerald levels. The growth is just fantastic. Another aspect of this is that we identify leaders more quickly; they are the ones who eagerly follow the pattern of success that they have seen. So the momentum just continues.'

Robert's eyes lit up as he described some of the members of the group of whom he genuinely felt so proud. 'We have a chap who used to be a shop floor worker in a shoe factory; another who runs a garage spares shop; there's another who was a clerk and is now full time in Amway; another couple are a J.P. and an industrial relations consultant and so on and so on. And the great thing is that they all get on so well together—professional people, people with degrees, manual workers, Roman Catholics, Salvation Army members ... all sorts. Amway is a wonderful social leveller.'

'Coming back to you and Suzanne, Robert,' I said. 'What are the most important things you have got out of your Amway business?'

'We have given ourselves a material reward at each important stage of the business we have reached,' he replied. 'We keep a dream folder and as we realise each particular dream we take it out. When we became Ruby Direct distributors we bought ourselves a 3-litre Granada Ghia. At Pearl level we had the kitchen and bathroom completely remodelled. When we became Emerald Direct distributors we bought a new car. We could not own this house without Amway. Every time I come through the front door I know that we owe our nice home to the efforts we've put into Amway over the last few years. But we already have a new house in view out in the country. We are planning private education for our little girl.

'But I suppose the biggest thrill for us is being part of something of which we are terribly proud. The Company is one hundred per cent behind us all the way. They will always go the extra mile to help. What some of those guys like John Dodds and Stewart McArthur did in the early days is just incredible. We have the strongest possible emotional ties to Hugh and Lyn and our uplines. They are the ones who stuck with this business in the early days when it was really tough. Then, of course, there are

1. Amway Corporation President Rich De Vos with the then UK General Manager, John Dodds, at the opening of the new Milton Keynes HQ in 1979 (Courtesy Amway (UK) Ltd)

2. Corporation Men—Rich De Vos, President of Amway Corporation (*left*), Jay Van Andel, Chairman of Amway Corporation (*right*), Stewart McArthur, General Manager of Amway (UK) Ltd since 1981 (*below*) (Courtesy Amway (UK) Ltd)

3. Amway Convention 1982. Part of the Crowd in the National Exhibition Centre, Birmingham (Courtesy Amway (UK) Ltd)

4. Leadership Travel Seminars in Spain—1979 (*top*), 1980 (*centre*), 1981 (*bottom*) (Courtesy A. an
S. Taylor)

5. UK Diamond Direct distributors enjoying Diamond Forum in Monte Carlo (*above*) and attending an Amway-sponsored concert in London (*below*) (Courtesy J. and D. Lyons and Amway (UK) Ltd)

6. A few items from the Amway product range (Courtesy Amway (UK) Ltd)

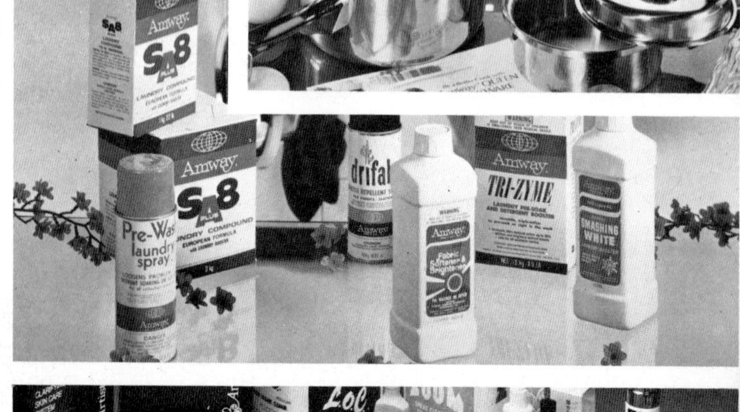

7. Amway (UK) Ltd offices and warehouse at Tongwell beside the M1 opened September 1982 (Courtesy Amway (UK) Ltd)

the people we've helped to their own success ... we love them all.'

*On the dream train*

Dennis and Barbara Rigg had been in their new house only a couple of weeks when I went to call on them. Petite, vivacious Barbara apologised for the mess but was obviously proud and happy for me to see her new dwelling. It was part of a rambling Victorian mansion, now divided into separate homes. 'We love old places,' she enthused in her delightful Lancashire accent. Dennis has designs on the next door homes; he wants to buy them up and knock the whole place back into one.'

I had travelled a short way up the M61 to find the outer suburb where the Haywards' close friends and colleagues lived. We settled in the attractive sitting room with its French windows giving onto a large garden. Dennis sat in a deep armchair and stretched his long legs. Barbara preferred a cushion on the polished wood-block floor. Dennis told me about the various occupations he had been involved in before Amway. They included being a sales rep, a builder's labourer and running a grocer's shop. 'The shop was a disaster,' Dennis explained. 'Not commercially—it was quite successful—but personally; it nearly split Barbara and me up. That was why, when we saw Amway—another business—Barbara didn't want to know. 'No,' his wife agreed. 'When we had the shop we were working seven days a week, twenty-three hours a day and Dennis had two part-time jobs besides—plus we had two tiny kiddies. The strain was just too much.'

They told me about the meeting at which they had been shown the Amway plan. 'Rob Hayward was showing it,' said Barbara. 'And I thought he was a con man, but I was very impressed with Suzanne because she is such a lady. The plan meant absolutely nothing to me so you can imagine how I felt when, at the end of the presentation, Dennis asked me for the family allowance money to buy a starter kit. I nearly hit the roof.' She laughed a shrill, infectious laugh. 'We had a flaming row—and he won.' 'Well,' he said, 'I thought it had to be worth a try. There was no risk involved and it might just work.'

Even then, they explained, it was only because other distributors coaxed them that they took the important step of going to a Business Expansion Programme in Birmingham, three months later. 'We very nearly quit several times,' Dennis told me. 'We sponsored a couple of people who only lasted a few weeks. We took meeting after meeting for one couple while they were in the pub!' Barbara exploded in another burst of laughter. 'We were that green,' she said. 'No wonder we had nothing to show for our efforts. But Rob kept telling us, "Whatever you put in will eventually come back to you many times over." We had just a faint glimpse of the possibilities. So we didn't give up. After BEP we went at it with a new zest and at last we started to get somewhere.' Dennis added, 'It was the challenge as much as the money that spurred us on—plus the realisation that the business was drawing us closer together. We decided that we were going to go Direct by Convention 1978 so that we could get our pins from Rich De Vos.' 'Oh that was a wondeful experience,' Barbara enthused. 'To actually be on stage with Rich is incredible. I don't think you really understand this business until you understand Rich and Jay's principles and the reason why Amway exists. Rich really motivates us; we love his principles and integrity.'

In 1980 the Riggs, with other local distributors started regular centre meetings in Bolton. They saw attendances grow from 40 to 400 in a few months. This was, as I had discussed with Rob Hayward, the early days of the 'North-west Explosion'. 'Well, we thought of that title,' said Barbara. 'We took the word "explosion" from an LP cover. We thought the group needed an identity. In those days it did. It needed to shout. It doesn't now. It's so large that its success is self-evident.'

Dennis went full time in June 1980. 'That was a bit too early,' he admitted, 'but it was great. And it gave us an incentive. Now we are at Emerald level and we have complete independence. We do what we want to do when we want to do it. We bought a Volvo and paid cash for it. We moved to this place from a terraced house.' Barbara added, 'But we don't just want success for ourselves. We both owe a lot to our parents and we want to be able to provide a bit extra for them now they're getting on. My Mum, for instance, has always dreamed of a thatched cottage with roses round the door. Well I'm going to give it to her. Then there are the children. Our business is in our wills for them. If anything happens to us they will be financially secure. And, of course, what's even more important, they are growing up with a positive mental attitude.'

'And that leads on to another of our dreams,' Dennis said. 'Because we have free time now and because we believe so strongly in the positive principles we've learned in the business, we want to spend some time with young people teaching them. We want to show them that life isn't as bad as many people seem to think. They can be successful. They can make a good future for themselves. We would like to run personal development courses for young people. It's not much use being successful if you don't share your success with others.'

Barbara smiled her wide, candid smile. 'You can see how many dreams we've got, can't you? We're on a sort of dream train and we're not going to get off.'

*Taking away the 'if only'*

The M62 wriggles free of Manchester and strikes up over the Pennines. I drove along it as dusk scooped black shadows out of the shallow valleys. Near Huddersfield I escaped from the motorway, took a snaking road round the hills and came at length to one of West Yorkshire's many granite villages. There, in a large house on a hillside overlooking a reservoir I found Michael and Mary Castell. They are a middle-aged professional couple who have brought up six children and are heavily involved in the life of the community. Mary is a magistrate. Michael, an accomplished violinist, is a leading figure in the musical activity of the area. Yet they have found time not only to build an Amway business but to build it enthusiastically to the Pearl level.

Mary and I talked in the spacious drawing room with the large windows looking out on the darkening hills while we waited for Mike to return from an orchestral practice. My hostess spoke lovingly, but not wistfully of earlier, better times. 'Michael inherited quite a bit of money from his father and we were pretty well off. We had our own farm and all that sort of thing. But most of that went into school fees and the expenses of bringing up a large family. We fondly imagined that when the children were off our hands we would be rich again. Inflation put paid to that dream. We found we were struggling to stay where we were let alone improve our way of life. Rather than resign ourselves totally to the inevitable, we started our own mail order business. That swallowed up about £7,000, and if we were going to save it we knew we'd have to pump in a hell of a lot more. By that time we had seen the Amway opportunity. We decided to cut our losses and concentrate all our efforts on Amway. At the beginning I saw it as a way of earning about £400 a month without working from nine to five. I didn't really appreciate the higher potential in the business.'

The Castells began with Amway in 1979 and built steadily. I asked Mary what their vision of the business was now. 'We certainly aim to go to the top—Crown and Crown Ambassador—and particularly we want a good international business in Europe and America,' she said. 'It's far too worthwhile a way of life ever to give up. We enormously enjoy meeting so many different kinds of people—and being able to help people. Round here at the moment there's so much redundancy, so many businesses going bust. We're in a position to say to those in difficulties, "Look, we've got something that will give you back your future." Because it really is about people, the one quality you have to acquire is the ability to build people up. That's quite hard work—but enormously worthwhile.'

I tried to probe gently, without using words like 'middle class', whether Mary had found any of the ideas in this American-based business alien in the early days. 'Oh yes, I had my cultural hang-ups,' she agreed disarmingly. 'I thought much of the first convention was awful. Then, when we went to training, and heard all about "defining your dreams" I thought it was a load of rubbish. Michael thought it quite fun and I remember getting cross when I found him cutting up my *Vogue* and *Harper's Bazaar* to get pictures for his dream folder. But of course I was wrong. Dreams are absolutely vital. You'll never build this business if you don't know what you want.'

At this point Michael bustled in, giggling over the latest political intrigues within the life of an amateur, provincial orchestra. I asked him what his first reaction to Amway had been. 'Oh, I didn't really believe it,' he said. 'But the figures intrigued me. I saw in them a fascinating mathematical exercise. I love problems and I spent ages trying to "crack" the plan, to find the fatal flaw in the argument.' Mary nodded. 'For the first three weeks whenever I did the washing I used to find pieces of paper with calculations on in all his pockets.' 'Eventually I had to accept that the plan was perfect,' John continued, 'Amway has certainly changed my thinking in a variety of ways. In my job in personnel management it's shown me just how negative many people are.' 'Yes, that comes home on the bench, too,' Mary added. 'People blame their parents, their circumstances, their background, anything but themselves. In this business you start where you are and, if you take a positive attitude, you can get to the top.'

Michael went out of the room in search of whisky and Mary talked awhile about her family. Tragedy had struck recently when one of their sons was killed in a road accident in Australia. 'That made me realise how important the family is. As it happened, most of us were together when the news arrived and we all drew enormous strength from that fact of being with each other. It strengthened my greatest Amway dream which is to have a large country house where all the children and grandchildren can come and feel they belong. It's that absence of a sense of belonging that lies behind so many of the problems I see in the courts.'

Michael came back and began filling and handing round glasses.

'What's the most exciting thing about Amway for you, darling,' his wife asked.

'The realisation that there's no limit to the size of business you can build,' he said.

'You know, *I* think, the most exciting thing is that Amway takes away those two sad little words "if only",' Mary said. 'So many people just stop trying. When most people get to fifty they give up. We've just reached our half century and we know that the second is going to be more exciting than the first.'

CHAPTER 8

# *Hope in Ulster*

I HAD never been frisked before. But then I had never made an air journey to Northern Ireland before.

The problems of Ulster came home to me personally while I was still on English soil. I stood in a little room at Birmingham airport, submitting to a body search and watching the contents of my case being expertly examined. Here I was travelling to another part of the United Kingdom, and discovering that security was tighter than on an international flight. It was an unnerving beginning to this section of my pilgrimage. Northern Ireland, as the world knows, is a country where terrorism and politico-religious conflict are ever-present realities. It is also a country, as the world, as yet, does not know, where Amway thrives. It was my task not to probe the reasons for the Protestant–Roman Catholic, Unionist–Republican struggle, but to see what difference a new business concept was making in the lives of individuals.

'Most people here are getting on leading their own lives,' John Lyons said. 'We're all affected by the troubles one way or another, whether we like it or not, but we're more concerned, on a daily basis, with earning our bread and butter and bringing up our kids.'

We were sitting in the restaurant at Belfast Airport and I was being treated to a very welcome 'Ulster Farmhouse' breakfast by a moustached, besuited man in his late forties. John Lyons is a Diamond Direct distributor who, until a couple of years ago, worked in an office in the centre of the city but who now savours complete liberty. He and his wife Diane divide their free time between frequent trips abroad and their spacious house at Donnaghadee with its views across the sea to distant Scotland. The thing that has changed their lives is, of course, Amway.

As we munched our bacon, eggs and potato cakes John told me about the job he had left behind. 'It was very much a routine task, very unrewarding, very unfulfilling. At the same time it had responsibilities and frustrations—so much so that I developed not one ulcer but two. My health was generally way, way down. I would often be off work for three or four days at a stretch. And whenever I looked forward I couldn't see life becoming any different—just another twenty years of to-and-froing through heavy traffic to get to an office to do something I didn't enjoy.'

The Lyons heard about Amway direct from the USA when a nephew of theirs, Glen Shoffler, wrote about it. He followed up the letter with a visit and that, in itself, impressed John.

'The fact that someone was prepared to come all the way, at his own expense, just to tell me about a business idea had to prove something. So we listened and we joined and Glen took two or three meetings to show some of our friends and we went 21% in the first month. It was as simple as that. We went Direct in the first three months and, by then, two of our own distributors had also reached 21%. We established good momentum right at the beginning.

We finished our meal in an unhurried way (John is an unhurried, unflappable type of person) and made our way to the car park. Outside the terminal building a little, grey-haired man hailed John and hurried up to engage him in conversation. 'Do you know what he wanted?' John asked as we fell into step once more. 'He wanted to join the business. That happens more and more these days. People are approaching us. The time may come when we hardly need to go out and find people at all.'

We drove in John's Mercedes through Belfast, out into the rolling meadows and eventually reached the one-time fishing town of Donnaghadee. There, in their lovely, modern, well-appointed house I met Diane, the other half of this highly successful partnership. Over a cup of tea—the first of many I was to drink during my stay—I asked them how they explained the rapid growth of their business. 'Right from the beginning we were taught by our sponsors the importance of really caring for people,' Diane said. 'Unless you're really prepared to become involved with your distributors and do all you can to help them achieve their success there's no point in getting involved in Amway. I suppose we've always been the sort of couple that people tend to turn to when they're in trouble, but we still had to learn a lot. This is what really impressed me when Glen showed us the business. He actually stood in front of a room full of people and told us he loved his wife. Then, when we went over to the States, we seemed to find that all the couples at high levels in the business had the same sort of beautiful relationship. I wanted that and Amway has given it to us. Now John and I are the best of friends. Before, we were just married.' John took up the theme. 'We stress how important it is for people to get things together as a couple before they can get their Amway business together. Time and again distributors come up to us and tell us that their marriages have improved since they started in the business.'

I asked what other reasons they had for going into Amway. 'One of my burning desires was to get over to the States to visit relatives,' said John. 'We achieved that within six months. We spent Christmas 1978 in America. We've been back several times since, sometimes on holiday, sometimes to visit Ada, speak at conventions and so on.' 'Once we were flown to Ada in one of the Amway executive jets,' Diane added. 'That was fabulous. Another dream realised for me was being able to take all four children on a skiing holiday last Christmas.' 'Our travels read like a tour operator's brochure,' John said. 'We've been to Canada, North Africa, Spain, Holland, Austria. There have been times when we've arrived home with barely enough time to repack our cases and fly out again.'

'We've recently got back from Diamond Forum in Monte Carlo,' Diane told me. 'That really is something else—sheer luxury. The food and service are superb. We had a marvellous trip across the Med. in a beautiful yacht. I won a few pounds in the Casino. We mixed with the great and the famous. There was a candlelit barbecue—oh, you just can't imagine what it was like.' 'Then, apart from travel,' John went on, 'there's this house. We moved here last year from a "semi" in Bangor. Four years ago we couldn't even have dreamed of living in a home like this. There were six of us living together on one wage packet.'

With the income, the freedom and the lifestyle they now enjoyed I suggested that they must have very few ambitions unfulfilled. 'Not a bit of it,' John insisted. 'New horizons open up all the time as you progress in the business. Things become possible that we didn't even know existed a few years ago. You see, it takes a while to realise that the sky really is the limit in this business. You can literally have anything you're prepared to work for.'

'Doesn't that mean,' I suggested, 'that you have to artificially whip up desires for more possessions in order to maintain momentum?' John shook his head. 'When all our dreams are fulfilled there are so many other people who have needs that we can help to meet. One thing we'd love to do is fund a mission hospital in Africa. Now, that's the sort of dream that, at the moment, is unattainable but I know that we will achieve it. It's only a matter of time. You see, you can just go on expanding your dreams without limit. I don't think most people can even envisage that.'

'Our biggest dream at the moment is to see all the people we've personally sponsored reach Diamond level,' Diane said. 'That will be really fulfilling. And it will happen very soon. Some of them will go Diamond faster than us because they have the advantages of the training programme, the books and the tapes that weren't all available when we started.'

I knew how important the 'PMA' books were to the Lyons because I had seen several on their shelves along with various religious and devotional books that told me, also, of their Christian faith. Coming along in the car John had explained his attitude towards material possession. 'If God wants you to be rich it's for a purpose. Nothing we have is ours. It's all from God and we have to find out how he wants us to use it.'

The Lyons were certainly generous with their hospitality towards me. During the time I spent with them there was a procession of visitors to the house—distributors collecting orders, distributors coming for help and advice, distributors who had been invited to meet me and tell their stories.

### *The man who should have died*

Harry Cunningham's story is one of the saddest, most tragic I have ever heard. It is also one of the most inspiring. As he sat in his wheelchair, eyes sparkling, face radiant with a happy, peaceful smile it was difficult to realise that he had lost the use of his legs. His whole body seemed so alert and vital. Yet Harry is a man who has been through intense physical and mental anguish.

Some years ago he was being driven to work in a minibus which lost a wheel and went out of control. In jumping clear, Harry caught his clothing on the door handle and was dragged along the ground beside the careering vehicle. When rescuers reached him his body was a smashed mess. He was virtually blind, was cut to pieces and had severe spinal injuries. Survival from the shock of the accident seemed impossible. But survive he did. He was blind, paralysed in both legs and his left arm, but he was alive. Doctors told him that, with such severe injuries, he could not expect to live more than three years. They reckoned without Harry's sheer guts. With determination and faith as his principal medication he forced his dimmed eyes to see again, his limp left arm to recover its strength. The dream that inspired him was a simple one, but intensely powerful. 'I wanted to escape the embarrassment of having other people dress and undress me and take me to the bathroom. I thought that if I could achieve that I wouldn't mind if my legs didn't work.' Achieve it he did. He could manoeuvre his wheelchair, return home and be independent.

But Harry's troubles were far from over. While he was in hospital a favourite brother died of lung cancer. Shortly after his discharge two other brothers also died. He had been home only three weeks when his wife was killed in a road accident. 'At that time,' Harry said 'I didn't care whether I lived or not. I could see nothing ahead of me but loneliness and for someone like me, who loves being with people, that was a terrible prospect.'

Some friends persuaded Harry to go on a trip to the famous shrine at Lourdes, where many miracle cures have reputedly been experienced. Harry certainly found healing there, though certainly of a kind he did not expect. It came in the form of a pretty, young ex-nun called Helen. 'She helped me put the broken pieces of my life together again. Helen is the best thing that's ever happened to me.' I scarcely needed Harry to tell me that. Looking at the slim, dark woman, with her roguish Irish smile, and seeing the glances the two of them constantly exchanged, I could have no doubts about the deep love that existed between them.

Harry and Helen were soon married and living in Kilkeel, Co. Clair. Helen gave up her nursing job to spend all her time looking after her husband. Life was not easy. They only had a disability pension to live on and the fast-dwindling compensation from the accident. Harry was frustrated because he could not earn a living and he felt guilty about keeping a young wife cooped up at home all the time when she could have been out meeting lots of other people.

It was after they had been married four years that they were shown the Amway plan. 'I didn't understand it at all,' said Harry. 'I thought the chap who showed us made his commission by selling starter kits. So we bought one just to help him out. We threw it into a cupboard and thought no more about it. But our sponsor asked us to arrange some meetings. So we did. We had a run of seven meetings. Each time we filled our living room with people. And each time they couldn't get away quick enough. As you can imagine, that depressed us. We did nothing for six months. During that time John and Diane came to visit us and explained more fully what Amway was all about. Then we sat down one day and really discussed it and I said, "Helen, is there any point in half measures? Let's either get in or get out." So we really became committed. We set up more meetings and showed the plan ourselves. Six weeks later we reached 21%. Now we are Direct distributors and that's only the beginning. If Helen was the best thing that's ever happened to me, Amway is certainly the second best. Now we are earning a good living. We're working together. We're meeting lots of people and helping lots of people.'

I asked Helen why she thought they had been suddenly so successful in the business. 'Because we suddenly saw the real possibilities. As soon as we believed in Amway our belief shone out to others. John and Diane helped us enormously. They're super people. We can't speak too highly of them. They gave us a real belief in ourselves and took us to seminars and rallies.'

'Amway has changed my life enormously,' she went on. 'I had always led a very sheltered life, first in the convent and then alone with Harry. I was very nervous of meeting people. Now I love it. The business has also changed my relationship with Harry. I restricted him before. I saw him as someone to be looked after. Now I see him as a person.'

Another point occurred to Harry. 'For years I couldn't go to church,' he said. 'It wasn't that there was anything physically preventing me; I just felt too embarrassed. I had a guilty conscience about not going but I just couldn't do it. Amway has given me the confidence to overcome that. Now I look forward to Sundays.' His face lit up in a wide smile in which there was yet a hint of frustration. 'Oh, if only I could get more people to realise what the Amway business can do for them. It has taken away my bitterness, loneliness and timidity and opened my life up to other people. Our lives are built round other people.'

I asked them about the future and they told me that they planned to reach Diamond level in 1983. They will use their increased income to have a new house built for them, and Harry, who used to be a trawlerman, would love to own his own yacht. But these were not the things that were really spurring them on as Harry explained. 'Those material possessions will come. What we really want, above all else, is to set up a home for homeless children. It may sound a big dream but I know, because I've proved it, that if you set out with a positive attitude you can achieve the impossible. Once I was told I'd never be able to lift a teaspoon with my left hand.'

*Why does someone rich and successful need Amway?*

Victor and Irene Irwin, whom I also met on my visit to Northern Ireland, are determined people, too, though they have a very different story to tell. Victor, smartly and expensively dressed, looked every inch the successful businessman he is. There was a dynamism about him, relayed in the ready Puckish smile and the way he sat forward in his chair, punctuating his remarks with short, stabbing hand movements. He is balding and of slender build. I put him in his late thirties. Nine years ago, he told me, without any capital of his own, he had started a construction and engineering business. He borrowed £160, hired machinery, and went to work. In the first year he had a £9,000 turnover. Now he has increased that to three quarters of a million. In the beginning he was on his own. Now he employs twenty men.

'We worked hard to build up to that level. It meant putting in long hours and every scrap of capital we could find. But we enjoy a challenge and it was very satisfying to see our labours crowned with success. Then two years ago recession hit the building industry and we were nearly put out of business. Well, we decided we were winners, not losers and that we would simply have to build everything up again. We worked harder than ever before. I used to start at five in the morning and usually didn't stop till ten or twelve at night. And, of course, Irene was a hundred per cent behind me in everything I did.'

I looked at the small, pretty, copper-haired young woman beside him and asked her about those years. 'They weren't easy,' she said. 'The house was always full. Even before we had our own children we had Victor's younger brother and sisters to look after, because his parents are dead. There were many times when we hadn't a pound in the house but we just went on and it was well worth it. Eventually we were able to build ourselves a lovely house.' She described to me the spacious dwelling in its own grounds, every detail of which had been planned with care and excitement. 'It's just been valued for us at £100,000,' Victor added.

My next question was obvious.

'Why does someone so successful need Amway? You have a flourishing business and an excellent income. Even if you sold up you would have enough to keep you in comfort to the end of your days.'

There was no hesitation about the reply.

'The business world involves constant hassle. We have constant difficulty getting money out of people. We have accumulated bad debts. We have problems with the labour force. People are constantly letting us down, not turning up for work, and so on. Now, when we were shown the Amway plan what we saw in it was freedom—freedom from all that hassle. We set ourselves the target of going Diamond in two years with a secure income that would enable us to do whatever we want with the building business. It's the freedom we see, not the money—freedom to meet people and spend a lot of time with them. That will mean work, but we've always been workers. Why not put in another two years in order to be able to have whatever we want thereafter?'

I asked them how long they had been in Amway. 'Four months,' said Victor. 'We have just reached 21% and we will be Direct distributors in another three months. We're very new in the business but we know enough to realise that Amway is the best business in the world. Already I've been able to start cutting back my construction business. I want to get it to the level at which I can manage it easily.'

'That's very important,' Irene added. 'I want Victor to be free of worry. In these days we have all sorts of problems over cash flow. It will be nice to know that we can write a cheque whenever we need to. Apart from that it's an exciting business and although we work hard it's so enjoyable that it really doesn't seem like work. And we run the business from home so we can spend time with our four children.'

I asked Victor if his previous business experience helped him. 'Well, Amway is a business anyone can run, who really wants to,' he replied. 'But where I think my past experience has helped is that I know no business ever runs smoothly. I realise there will be setbacks and challenges to overcome. So when I meet downlines who tell me after a month or two that they're quitting I can put them on the right lines. I tell them that no businessman ever started something up and only gave it a few weeks to succeed. O.K., perhaps they have no previous business experience. Then, it may take them a little bit longer to develop the right attitude. But, it's only a few who get despondent. Most of them share our excitement. We've found a business that gives us a lot of happiness and contentment and that is such a contrast with anything we've known before.'

Irene said, 'Let me give you a concrete example. A while back Victor's firm resurfaced the drive for our church. We didn't want to take the money for that, but because of our cash flow situation we had to. Soon we shall be able to give that £4,000 back to the church, and that will give us such a thrill. That's the sort of difference Amway makes.'

### *He left in a gold Rolls-Royce*

'The last thing I wanted was Amway, or anything else that would take Dave away from home. He was already out several nights a week. He played in a pop group and he was selling insurance in his spare time. I hardly ever saw him.'

Pat McCune, an attractive young blonde, told me about her initial reactions to the Amway plan. 'We sat in this couple's house and saw the business. I had a closed mind and I thought Dave wasn't interested because he never said a word all evening. We got home and I went to bed but he stayed up. When I went to see what he was doing I found him making out a list of friends and relations who might be interested in Amway, and he simply said "We're joining".'

Dave McCune sat beside his wife on the sofa chuckling. He is a young man with a round face, ample moustache and dark, smiling eyes. He told me why his response had been so immediate. 'I was working in the computer department of a large tobacco firm and I wanted to get out and run my own business. I was actually looking for something when the Amway opportunity came along. Straight away I said to myself "This is it. There could be a lot of money in this.' I saw it as a means of giving up my job. I suppose like most other men in Britain I had accepted the first employment that came along paying reasonable money. It was O.K. as jobs go but I didn't relish the thought of staying in it for the rest of my working life.'

Dave started his Amway business in June 1979, determined to succeed even though his wife gave him no active support. It took Pat six months to realise that there might be something in this Amway thing. 'I kept getting enquiries at home,' she said. 'Excited wives who had a dream and who were beginning to get somewhere in the business. They were asking me questions and I didn't know the answers. So I sat down and thought about it. I identified my own dreams and I learned about the business so that I could help these people whom Dave had signed up.'

Once Dave and Pat were really pulling together things moved fast. They set themselves a goal of reaching the Diamond level in two years and, in fact, hit their target in two years and two months. Dave gave up his pop group and his insurance to devote more time to Amway, and they gave their business the bulk of their free time. It paid off handsomely. Just over two years from starting in Amway Dave gave up his job at the factory. It was quite an occasion.

'I had taken quite a bit of leg-pulling at work from people who made fun of my soap-selling. They used to call me 'Buzby' because I was on the phone so often. So I wanted to show those people; I wanted to have the last laugh. First of all I thought of getting a helicopter to come and collect me inside the works but that was ruled out because of the security situation in this country. The next best thing was a Rolls-Royce. So I hired a gold coloured Rolls with a chauffeur to pick me up from the factory gate. I came out with my mates and then watched their mouths fall open as the door of this gorgeous car was held open for me and I was driven off, giving them the royal wave as I went.'

I asked them what other things they had got out of the business and what their unfulfilled dreams were. 'We're at the moment having a large bungalow built on a prime site,' Dave said. 'We have a new Mercedes estate car on order and Pat is driving her dream car, a Jaguar XJS. We've travelled a great deal. Most of our material dreams have been realised. In the future I want to record some of my songs. I write quite a few songs and I'd like to have them put on disc by a really good group. But the greatest thing is having the freedom to see our children grow up.' 'Yes,' Pat added, 'that and having a common interest. When Dave was working in computers we had little to talk about. I was actually thinking about finding a job, not only because we needed the money but because he seemed to be out of the house all the time and I didn't see why I shouldn't be out, too. Now we have a business to plan together.' The sun glinted on her golden hair as a slight shiver ran through her. 'Sometimes I think how close we came to missing this business. If Dave had listened to me and given up ... Now there's no way we're going to give up.'

Who was it said 'Diamonds are forever'?

The time eventually came for me to leave. Once again John Lyons and I were eating our 'Ulster Farmhouse' breakfasts at Belfast Airport. I thanked him for all his help and the hospitality he and Diane had extended to me. He smiled. 'In return,' he said, 'Will you, please, make one thing clear in your book? It's this: anyone coming into this business should have no doubts about it. I am convinced that Amway is going to be the biggest corporation in the world in a very few years and most of that growth will be outside the USA. Thousands and thousands and thousands of people are going to have their lives improved by it. On the other hand I have never heard of anyone who has come to any harm through Amway.'

We said our goodbyes. I went off to be frisked again and to board my 'plane. As the 1-11 soared over the green meadows of Ulster I realised that I had seen no soldiers, no processions, no burnt-out cars, no evidence of Ireland's bloody history. It had all been there in the background. People I spoke to had made occasional references to the 'troubles'. Yet their main preoccupation was with a successful present and a future full of promise. That was a hopeful sign.

CHAPTER 9

# *Interaction in Scotland*

RUNAWAY lovers who reached Gretna Green to be wed over the anvil had probably given ample proof of their mutual devotion by the mere act of enduring the journey. It is a long drive to Scotland even by motorway. In a bygone age it was certainly longer, uncomfortable and hazardous, particularly so towards journey's end. The country on either side of the border was for centuries desolate and lawless. As I followed the squirming A74 through Annandale, past hillsides blocked out with conifer plantations, it took little imagination to envisage hordes of half-clad 'reivers' careering down to the roadside brandishing swords and screeching war cries. These tracts of wildly beautiful country have seen more skirmishes and battles than any other part of Britain.

But all was peaceful as I continued north, then swung off the dual carriageway to drive through quiet old villages towards the bustling new town of East Kilbride. This is the largest and, its inhabitants believe, most successful post-war development in Scotland. Planned as a complete community for 85,000 people, it serves every need of its inhabitants. Unlike nearby Glasgow, light industry flourishes and there is little unemployment. Housing areas, open spaces and shopping precincts are well laid out. Children (the average age in East Kilbride is 29) travel safely over footpaths and cycleways. Considerable thought has obviously been given to the citizens' physical well-being. Among those who take thought for their spiritual welfare is Jack Strachan, evangelist and minister in the Church of Christ.

I had come to see Jack because, as well as being involved full-time in a preaching and pastoral ministry, he is a Diamond Direct distributor, and a pioneer of the Amway business in Scotland with a total organisation of over 3,000, which calls itself the 'Strachan Interaction'.

I suppose the word 'evangelist' had inclined me to expect an aggressively hearty individual who might fix me with a penetrating gaze and ask me whether I was saved. In fact the door was opened to me by a Pickwickian figure—tubby, bespectacled and genial. Jack welcomed me warmly and introduced me to his wife, Maureen, who gave me a fresh, open-faced smile. We chatted happily for several hours and by the time I left I knew why this couple were so widely loved and respected within the world of Amway.

Their story began in 1978 when they were in a desperate situation. The financial support from their congregation was generous but the Strachan family was unable to keep up with inflation. New clothes for the children were rare. Holidays were non-existent. They were on the verge of having to sell their house. Maureen took a nightshift job to help out but the strain of this on top of the demanding life of a minister's wife was too great and she collapsed. It was at about this time that US visitors, Bruce and Betty Flannery, showed them the Amway opportunity. They saw it as literally a godsend. It seemed to be the answer to their prayers; the means of banishing financial worry and enabling them to get on with their church work. They were foster-sponsored by Al and Joyce Greaves and made an enthusiastic start. Then doubt set in. There were delivery problems. Other people suggested that the Corporation was not as honest as it made out. Some members of Jack's family were disturbed at the thought of a minister selling soap. So, one day in August 1980, Jack Strachan decided to quit. The kit and all the products in the house were packed up to be returned when the Amway van called. But it did not call that week. So Jack decided to go to a rally the following evening to hand in his resignation personally. The meeting was attended by about thirty people—most of the active distributors in Scotland at that time—and was addressed by Joyce Greaves. Jack described that meeting very vividly. 'Joyce spoke about the need for goals and she suddenly looked at me and said, "Jack, what's your goal?" Those next few seconds seemed like minutes. All kinds of thoughts chased through my mind. What I was really doing was taking a good, hard look at myself. I realised I was a quitter—and I can't stand quitters. After what seemed an age I got to my feet and I said "We're going 21% this month". Now, it was then half way through the month and we were at 12% but I'd made the commitment and we did it and we've never looked back since. Amway has taken away financial worry and thereby made my ministry more effective. The positive thinking I've learned in this business has helped enormously in my church work. Our family has a really good standard of living. We support a student at divinity school. We have increased our missionary giving. We take holidays when we need the refreshment. This year we're all going to the Holy Land—and that's a dream I've had for years. And we can help so many other folk we couldn't help before. For years I've ministered to people's spiritual needs but so often their difficulties are largely financial. Now, I can offer them Amway, a real opportunity to improve their lot.'

I suggested that some people might find something contradictory about a Christian leader becoming rich and urging other people to do so, too. He smiled and answered very quickly. It was obvious that he had faced up to that question before. 'The idea that Christians shouldn't make money is quite wrong,' he said. 'When I look in the Bible I find there are lots of wealthy people. And God used them and used their wealth. Having money is neither good nor bad. It's what you do with it that counts. Now we enjoy some of it ourselves and we use some of it to help others and both of those are good.'

I pushed him a little further. What about setting material dreams and goals, I said, did not that clash with the idea of trusting God for 'daily bread'? Jack's reply was equally prompt. 'God has made us in such a way that we only develop properly if we stretch ourselves, if we reach out for dreams and goals and achievements. As long as we have our priorities right and put him first then, I believe, there is nothing wrong with having material ambitions. In fact, we've helped a number of people to get rid of their hang-ups about possessions being wrong.'

What is clear is that the Strachans think very carefully about how they spend their money. Instead of an impressive car they would rather buy things which help other people or help the Strachans in their church work. 'At this time we could buy any house in East Kilbride,' Jack told me, 'but it's not right for us to move at the moment.' They are also restricted in their use of time. They will not work on Sundays and they only devote two evenings a week to Amway. They maximise this time, usually, by taking meetings separately so that they have four evenings between them. The fact that Amway definitely takes a second place in their lives makes their achievements even more remarkable. They were the first Scottish distributors to reach Diamond level. In the spring of 1982 they were able to hire Glasgow's famous Kelvin Hall for a rally of 1500 distributors. When we met they were in the process of organising a gigantic Amway family picnic at Strathclyde.

It is obviously their concern for people that contains the real secret of their success. When they were looking for a snappy title for their large organisation they came up with the name 'Strachan Interaction'. 'that really seemed to sum up what it's all about—people and groups interacting to help each other,' Jack explained.

On the wall of the Strachans' lounge is an attractive copper plaque of which they are very proud. It was sent to them by a young American student who stayed a while with them and whom they introduced to Amway. It says what many other people could also say:

Jack and Maureen
To the two people who changed my life by sharing a dream
I love you
Tommy Primm

*An excited evening at the Royal Scot*

Edinburgh Castle is a tiring place to explore. It spreads over the top of its rock and the visitor must struggle up many steps and climb steep paths of foot-punishing cobble if he is to probe every corner of this ancient fortress. It is a grim place—solid and well-fortified with many evidences of its long history as a garrison and prison. But at its pinnacle lies a small building of great beauty, simplicity and peace. St Margaret's Chapel is tiny and sparsely furnished—a whitewashed domed interior, a Norman arch with dog-tooth decoration leading to a small apse containing a table, supporting a vase of flowers. It is Edinburgh's oldest building. For eight and a half centuries it has borne witness to the stability of Christian devotion, while kings and queens, generals and captives, lairds and paupers, victors and vanquished have lived out their brief lives within yards of its thick walls. It is only six paces from the door of the chapel to the parapet from which the visitor can see much of the city spread out before him. Princes Street lies below and beyond a panorama of roofs, office blocks, spires and chimneys stretching to the Firth of Forth. I thought of the hundreds of thousands of people out there—shoppers and shopkeepers, employers and employees, teachers and learners, workers and unemployed. Here was I, I reflected, studying something I was finding increasingly fascinating and exciting, something that was changing the lives of many people, something destined to become a household word within a few years. Yet most of the people out there had never heard of Amway—just as so many inhabitants of the castle had remained oblivious to the message to which St Margaret's Chapel bore witness.

That evening I met a group of people who were working hard to rectify that situation. Gordon and Maureen Craig, Emerald Direct distributors, had promised to bring one or two Amway friends to meet me at the Royal Scot Hotel, where I was staying. I had not booked a room, feeling sure that it would be easy enough to find a corner where a few people could have a quiet chat. I waited in the foyer for my guests and at the appointed time Gordon and Maureen arrived. So did nine other people. A quiet chat? Out of the question when you have eleven excited and talkative Amway distributors all together. The only place I could take them to was my bedroom. We all crowded in and found seats on beds, chairs, stools and floor and there for a couple of hours or more they regaled me with a string of stories, jokes and anecdotes about Amway's growth in Scotland.

'There were distributors here in the early days,' someone said, 'but it wasn't really until Jack Strachan began to put his organisation together that anything really exciting started to happen. The Scots are pretty canny folk. They take some convincing.'

'Maureen and I certainly owe everything to Jack,' Gordon Craig told me. 'We married before we were ready for the responsibilities of marriage. For one reason or another I started drinking heavily. I made a mess of my life and I became impossible to live with. So Maureen and I parted company. Seven years later I met Jack Strachan and he pointed out to me the error of my ways. With his help I turned over a new leaf and kicked the drinking habit. It was some weeks later that he told me about Amway. He thought it would help me to have something else to think about besides my own problems. And he was right. I built my business to the Direct level in a year. Then I was able to pluck up courage to go back to Maureen and ask if we could try again. I felt that I was a reformed character, and that I had some solid achievement to show her.' Maureen took up the story. 'the first couple of times he wrote I didn't take any notice but then he asked me to meet him at his parents' house and within a few minutes he was showing me this new business he'd got into. I thought it was a bit odd at first but then I began to be impressed. Well, one thing led to another and I found I was experiencing a second courtship and I'd started in Amway at Direct distributor level. That wasn't easy. People kept asking me questions I couldn't answer. But as I got into the business I enjoyed it more and more and I just have to be grateful to Amway for helping to bring us back together.' Gordon resigned his job in the prison service at the beginning of 1981, giving up his house, pension and insurance but he has no regrets. 'Amway has given us a good income and the chance to spend our time building friendships and making a whole new future.'

'That's exactly the way we see it. A new future for us and, especially, James.' It was Jim Hayes, a smartly dressed man in his early forties who spoke. The others were nodding sympathetically, obviously knowing something that I did not know. 'Who's James?' I asked. 'He's our younger son,' Grace Hayes explained. He has a serious heart condition. He needs a lot of looking after. We love him very much but he has been a tie, especially for me. For years I hardly ever went out of the house and I met very few people. Amway has given us hope for him and for a better future for all of us. It was for James' sake we joined Amway in the first place. We thought we might be able to make enough money to get James a battery car so that he could get about more. When we reached 18% we bought him a car. James really enjoys Amway. He's met a lot of people. He comes to the rallies. He helps us with the business. He knows that Amway could make a real difference, not only with providing things we've never been able to give him but we may be able to afford new treatment in the future. Sometimes I go all hot and cold when I remember that, if I'd had my way we wouldn't have got into Amway at all.'

I asked how that was. It was Jim who told me the story. 'I'd been to see about getting an electric kettle repaired. I was sitting in my car outside afterwards when there came a tap at the window and there was this fellow in overalls standing there. And he says 'I was hearing what you were saying in there. You sound as though you could use some extra money. Perhaps I can help.' Now there was I—a civil engineer, smart suit, company car—and this truck driver comes up in grubby overalls, offering to show me how to make money. Anyway, eventually I gave him my phone number, and I never expected to hear any more. But that evening he phoned and asked if he could come round with his brother-in-law to show the business. So the two of them appeared and, as you can imagine, we were in no mood to be impressed. Anyway half way through Grace got up and said "I don't want to hear any more", and left the room. She was convinced it was pyramid selling. I wasn't very impressed either until these blokes asked if I knew John Hart, the architect, who was also in Amway. Now John and I had been at school together and were still quite friendly. So I contacted him and when he and Margaret came round we listened to the plan properly and were convinced, but, by golly, it was a close thing. Now, Chick Gray the "lorry driver" and his wife Audrey are two of our closest friends.'

I asked them all how far Amway had spread in Scotland. 'As far as Orkney and Shetland,' was the reply. They all began listing off their distributors' locations—Dundee, Aberdeen, the Highlands, the Isles. 'The organisation is strongest in the Lowlands,' Gordon commented. 'But that's only because we haven't yet spent the time to go farther afield to set up other flourishing centres,' someone added, and there was a murmur of assent.

There was no let-up in the conversation. These people were all happy, excited and believed totally in what they were doing. Clive Sutherland, a quiet young man, from Dundee had driven the fifty miles from his home after a busy day's work just to be with his Amway friends and share his experiences with me. Amway meant a lot to him, he said, 'because it's helped me to realise who I am and why I'm here.' He explained that for years he had been a painfully shy person. He worked as a landscape gardener, was unmarried and devoted almost all his spare time to constructing an enormous model train layout. Now, after a year in Amway, he and his parents had built to Direct distributor level and that had meant speaking at many meetings, becoming involved with lots of other people and helping them to be successful. 'My life will never be the same again. I've found the greatest business in the world and I'm going to stick with it.'

Quite different was the story of John and Margaret Hart. John is a successful architect and illustrator with his own practice. Margaret is a perfumery buyer. They were contemplating moving to the United States, where there were definite openings with wealthy clients, at the time he saw the Amway plan. At the second viewing all thoughts of emigration vanished. He and Margaret threw themselves into Amway instead and built to Direct level in five months. Now they can see the chance of John cutting down his business commitments and accepting only those commissions that really excite him, both here and overseas. Different again were another couple who belonged to this happy group of friends. Charlie and Helen Miller were not professional people. Amway evenings for Helen have replaced evenings she used to spend playing bingo. She was so excited about her new business that many of her friends clamoured to join, too.

It was late into the night before my guests left, leaving me to ponder on the kind of organisation that could bring together architects, manual labourers, prison officers, engineers, landscape gardeners, lorry drivers, ministers of religion and countless other people, as equal members of a team.

CHAPTER 10

# *Visionaries, Sceptics and A Very Angry Lady*

I STOOD alone amid the ruins of Rievaulx Abbey and thought about the power of dreams. The crumbled walls and broken pillars dominate peaceful Ryedale as they have since the last monks left four and a half centuries ago. Even then Rievaulx was ancient. Its first inhabitants had begun to set stone upon stone a further four hundred years back in time. The white-robed Cistercians who built their abbey in this lovely Yorkshire valley were impelled by a dream—though they would have called it a vision. The soaring pillars of their great church spoke of the splendour of God. The six hundred monks and lay brothers who spent their lives within its shadow were dedicated to pointing their fellow countrymen towards that same God. A callous King Henry VIII thought he could destroy that vision as easily as his agents stripped the lead from the roofs, emptied the treasury and carried away all that was valuable from Rievaulx. But the moss-covered stumps of columns and the glassless windows witness just as surely to the Lord of creation as the plainsong that once echoed round them.

What ensures such durability? Is it the subject of the vision or the ardour of the visionaries? My mind went back to the people I had met since recrossing the border into England. They were dreamers and obviously devoted dreamers. The previous evening I had attended a 'centre meeting' at a hotel on the outskirts of Middlesbrough. The room held about eighty people and it was filled mainly with 'young marrieds', members of John and Margaret Cundall's group, and friends they had brought to the fortnightly get-together, to hear the sales and marketing plan, watch an Amway film, and meet some of their fellow distributors. Few of those distributors had progressed far in the business; they were still serving their novitiate (to stick with the monastic metaphor). Yet it seemed their belief was total. Afterwards they packed and overflowed the hotel bar where the staff were rushed off their feet. 'They never learn,' someone muttered cheerfully as he edged past with a trayful of drinks. 'They ought to know by now that they need more people serving on Tuesdays.' Among those I spoke to were Barry and Barbara Smith, a couple in their late twenties. Wedging himself into a corner and raising his voice above the chatter of the throng, Barry explained that, as an accountant, he had been unimpressed with the Amway scheme when he first saw it. 'When you spend your working day dealing with large figures, the sort of amounts they put in the circles don't excite you.' He had looked very carefully into the Company's financial and legal background and had been unable to find anything wrong with it. So, rather reluctantly, he and Barbara had joined. 'We didn't really need Amway,' he explained. 'I was doing rather well as a company accountant with a large firm. Then, all of a sudden, the firm went bust and I was out of a job. Fortunately, I managed to find another one; I was lucky. But that experience made me think. Now Amway gets all the time Barbara and I can give it, and the sooner we can pack in our other jobs and rely solely on ourselves, within the world of Amway, the happier I shall be.'

Barry's words came back to me as I surveyed Rievaulx Abbey from the hillside above. What a self-sufficient, isolated world the monastery had been. So many of the men who had lived here had deliberately sought refuge from the feudal anarchy of medieval society; from the barons who exacted heavy taxes, the petty armies which trampled crops, the economic uncertainty that made it hard for a merchant to earn a satisfactory living, the bands of thugs who waylaid travellers and broke into honest men's homes. The abbey offered them escape from all that and an atmosphere in which they could pursue their own vision with others of a like mind. Was it a similar attraction that Amway held for couples like the Smiths? Few people in Britain in the 1980s believe in the ability of governments or industrial management to arrest economic decline. The concept of a 'secure job' is virtually a thing of the past. There are therefore not many citizens of these islands who can plan their future with any degree of confidence. In Amway some of them seem to have found a sanctuary from economic chaos and the social chaos which dogs its heels. Within its free enterprise walls they can rely on themselves to attain their dreams and also know the warm encouragement of other members of a community dedicated to the same objectives.

I turned my back on the ruins and walked slowly down the short drive to the car park. Critics of the monasteries had always denounced them as inward-looking and escapist communities whose inmates turned their backs on the real problems of the world to enjoy personal security, indolence and even, in some cases, luxury. Those who upheld the religious life claimed that, on the contrary, monks and nuns undergirded contemporary society with their prayers and preserved spiritual and cultural values which would otherwise have been lost. As I climbed into the car I was still playing the game of superimposing the world of Amway on the ancient Cistercian way of life. Were these Amway folk escapists or dedicatees to a deeper reality? It was something we had talked about the night before in the hotel bar. I had heard the story of a man in the Cundalls' group who worked as a crane-driver. He was made redundant and, shortly afterwards, joined Amway. One of the first things he did was try to interest the sales manager of his old firm in starting an Amway business. The executive was impressed, not only with the business but with the enterprise shown by the ex-employee. The end result was twofold; Amway gained a new recruit and the crane-driver got his job back. That certainly seemed to indicate some kind of ideological feedback from Amway into the established system.

'The way I see it,' said a tie-less, curly-haired young man, clutching a glass of scotch, 'the poor can't help the poor. We all know people with problems and ninety per cent of them boil down to money in the end. Well, if you're struggling to make ends meet yourself there's not much you can do for them.' 'Do you see the successful Amway person as someone who goes around dishing out charity,' I asked provocatively. He was unabashed. 'Wherever I can give any help, I will, but I think it's far more important for people to see me succeed. They can look at me and say "If he can do it so can I". Then they can use Amway to get over their financial problems by their own efforts. That way they preserve their self-esteem.'

The car meandered through the tiny hamlet of Rievaulx, climbed the hill, turned a bend and the abbey site was lost to view. I indulged my flight of fancy for a couple of minutes longer. What can the individual do in a troubled society? The Cistercians' answer had been a twofold one like that of my friend in the bar—practise charity and point men to a better way. I regained the main road and headed south.

### *A bit 'snobby'*

'I think I must have been a bit snobby. We had a respectable, well-established family business and here was somebody trying to interest us in a direct-selling deal.' As she spoke Margaret Cundall was surrounded by piles of Amway boxes from which she was compiling orders for her many distributors.

John and Margaret run a pharmacy in a quiet suburb of Middlesbrough. They have a pleasant home and five children whose ages range from seven to eighteen. John has the qualities which obviously make him a successful provincial shopkeeper: he is cheerful, quiet, reliable, discreet. Sitting in his comfortable lounge and reflecting on the beginnings of their Amway enterprise, he appeared thoughtful, almost diffident. A few hours later I saw him showing the sales and marketing plan to a roomful of people in a nearby hotel. He looked much the same. As he made his points on a blackboard, there was no skilful oratory, no excited arm waving, no gimmick; just a straightforward, take-it-or-leave-it explanation. If the Cundalls are much respected and loved, as clearly they are, by the many people they have introduced to Amway, it is obviously for their quiet, dependable, genuine concern to help and serve other people.

Margaret explained to me how they had needed a great deal of persuading to join Amway. They were rather suspicious about it. They reckoned that their pharmacy and their family kept them quite busy enough. Their own business was successful and provided what seemed a good standard of living. Anyway, selling cosmetics, soaps and shampoos privately could only be cutting their own throats as conventional retailers. However, John was eventually convinced enough to give it a try, and Margaret went along, though she made it quite clear that she was not prepared to canvass her friends until she was quite sure that it would work. 'As I got into the business,' she explained, 'my hesitation soon disappeared and I was happy to talk to anyone about it.'

I was interested in those words. I wanted to know how someone whose livelihood was derived from selling across the counter could be 'happy' to get involved in a business whose motto was 'Shop without going shopping', and one of whose rules explicitly forbade marketing through commercial retail outlets. When I asked Margaret if this worried her at all, she shook her head. 'Not really,' she said. 'The only area of conflict is soap and cosmetics and the Amway goods are better than the lines we carry in the shop.' I asked her if she felt able to approach other retailers with the Amway opportunity. 'Oh yes,' she replied. 'In fact people in retailing or other kinds of selling often grasp the plan much more quickly than people with no commercial background.' 'And they can quickly see that Amway has certain advantages,' John added. 'One reason I like it is that I don't have to tie up capital in it. In the shop we've just spent a lot of money up-dating the premises. By the time we've regained that investment, the shop will probably need more cash spent on it. These are hard times for the small shopkeeper. Supermarkets and hypermarkets are stealing more and more trade. Government regulations and restrictions are always on the increase. Life is very frustrating.' He believed that Amway provided an excellent opportunity for the 'little man' to hit back at the system; to operate a very simple business based on products which were more economical than those provided in the big stores. 'Are you tired of the pharmacy?' I asked. John laughed. 'At times I could cheerfully chuck it all up, it gets that frustrating,' he said. 'But I must confess that basically I love it. What we aim to do is build our Amway business until it's providing us with enough income for us to put someone else in charge of the pharmacy. Then we shall be able to come and go as we please, spend much more time with the children, take longer holidays, and so on.'

John and Margaret have worked hard on building their local group. They were full of stories about distributors who, with varying degrees of success, were working the Amway scheme. It had been their major aim, they explained, to create a happy environment which people would enjoy and which would help build up group loyalty. They had started fortnightly centre meetings and quarterly rallies. As a result the group was growing rapidly and soon they would need a new rally venue because the local hotel where they met could hold only about four hundred. They believed it was worthwhile in the early stages to plough back some of their profits into ensuring growth but, after a couple of years in Amway, they do have a new car and other perks to show for it. They are also the centre of an ever-widening circle of happy, positive people.

I discovered this at the centre meeting that night. It was late by the time I had extricated myself from the throng of excited distributors, each of whom seemed bent on telling me how wonderful Amway was. You cannot help but be impressed by such a gathering and I still had a warm glow inside me next morning when I set out to drive across the moors to Humberside.

### *A sceptic*

Norman Lees is a sceptic, although he prefers the word 'realist'. He had a scientific training, spent all his working life in laboratories, believed only in facts that could be proved, and loved a good, academic argument. His wife, Jenny, despaired of him socially. 'I could never take him to parties,' she said. 'He always ended up in a corner with half a dozen other men locked in deep discussion over the quantum theory or some such. Other wives had to physically drag their husbands away from him.'

I had come to Goole because people said 'you must meet the Lees; they've had fantastic growth'. I found an intelligent couple with soft northern accents and two teenage sons. From what I had been told I might have expected a bubbling, dynamic, effervescent couple. If I did not expect that it was because I had learned very early on not to anticipate what sort of people I would meet in Amway. I had had too many surprises. I now kept an open mind. Norman and Jenny Lees are a quiet, cheerful and obviously very thoughtful couple. 'We don't build our group on enthusiasm and razzamatazz; we build it on sound business principles,' Norman said, polishing his spectacles, and he was soon quoting me figures and percentages to prove his point. Given the Lees background, this is the only way they can operate. Norman was, until recently, a Senior Scientific Medical Officer and Jenny was a teacher. They are the sort of people who cannot bear to be mentally inactive. They are keen cyclists with an interest in races and rallies. A couple of years ago Norman took an Open University degree, in order to stave off boredom.

It was boredom that drove him into Amway. There was not enough stimulus in his job. He was underemployed. He did not like the people he was working with. 'Frankly, it was driving me round the bend. I mean that quite seriously. I used to suffer from severe bouts of depression. And what made it worse was that I could see no prospect of getting out.' One day their younger son, Grant, was invited to a meeting to hear about a business opportunity. His parents strongly urged him not to go but the lad was determined. When Grant came home and tried to tell Norman and Jenny what he had learned about Amway, Norman's reaction was, 'No son of mine is selling soap'. The next day he started reading some of the literature Grant had brought back, submitting it to close scrutiny, determined to expose Amway for the fraud it had to be. When, after a week, he had found no flaw, his own dedication to logic forced him to the conclusion that Amway was probably sound. And if it was true that this 'soap business' could provide a key to financial independence then it was exactly what he needed to escape from the drudgery of his laboratory work. Having proved that point to his own satisfaction, this realist signed an application form and started an Amway business. The date was 8 November 1980. On 8 November 1981 the doors of Norman Lees' hospital laboratory closed behind him for the last time and he took his first deep breaths of air as a free man.

The preciseness of the timing was symbolic. It characterised the Lees' whole approach to their new business. They planned their growth carefully. They would deploy their natural abilities; Norman would do the planning and Jennifer would specialise in personal contacts. They worked hard and they flashed past the Amway lap markers like cyclists with their eyes on the finishing post. By the end of three months they had reached the 21% level. A month later they had passed the Ruby level, thus reaching a higher level than Direct before completing their three months qualification as Direct distributors. The momentum that Norman and Jenny had built up carried on throughout their group. 'Other people thought our growth rate was the norm, so they matched it.' I had plenty of evidence of that during the evening I spent with them. There was a constant stream of telephone calls and visitors—distributors placing or collecting orders or reporting on sponsoring meetings. One friend called in on his way to Scotland where he had a flourishing group of his own to speak to. Norman and Jenny numbered off on their fingers a dozen or so people in their group who either were or were about to become Direct Distributors. As they did so the pictures stuck on their sitting room door began to make sense to me.

There, for themselves and any visitors to see, was a chart of the upper Amway levels. Against each level a date was written. It culminated in 'Crown, Feb. 1985'. 'That's not wishful thinking; that's planning,' said Norman. 'We've done the ground work. We've already got a solid base. The way we're helping downline and providing training ensures that Directs will keep on breaking.' I commented that they seemed to have everything so well organised that they must have been Amway naturals before they joined. They laughed. 'Oh, no, we've learned a lot,' said Jenny. Norman added, 'Do you know the thing that was hardest for me to learn was belief. It's difficult for a realist to admit that if you really believe something, it'll happen. But we've proved it now so often. Early on in this business we looked at some of the people wearing the bigger pins, and we said, "We may think we know better but these are the successful ones. We'll do it the way they say." And it worked! We've set ourselves goals and we've really believed we could achieve them. And we have.'

Certainly everything is going swimmingly for the Lees at the moment. Their first Amway year gave Norman independence and a new car. And Jennifer? What had she got out of it? 'Well, the most important thing is a pleasanter man to live with!' She plans to give up teaching soon. 'It'll be a wrench; I love my work. But there are all sorts of travel opportunities opening up for us and there's no way that I'm going to be left behind.' I asked them what else they plan to do with their increasing income. Norman appeared quite blasé about the future. 'I'm not very materialistically minded. We're going to do this place up and sell it. Then we'll move into a bigger house. All the trappings of success will obviously come but they don't concern me very much. There's only one thing I want—and I want it passionately. That's to build the biggest Amway business in this country.'

I did not tell him he would have plenty of competition. I was sure he already knew that. I was also sure that this convinced realist had taken the fact fully into account.

*A very angry lady*

It was Karen getting upset with her father that really set the ball rolling, for, as Dennis Peacock explained, 'When you get Karen upset you've got one very angry lady on your hands.'

Terry and Karen McCollin had been in the Amway business a couple of years by the time that memorable Christmas came along. Her parents had come over from Denmark for the festive season and during the course of the holiday her father made the unguarded remark, 'Oh, you're not still in that soap business, are you? That'll never work.' Karen stifled her rage as best she could but she decided that, come hell or high water, she would prove her scoffing parent wrong.

In 1980 the McCollins invited Karen's mother and father to come and live near them in England and to manage an export business which they had established. This meant a great deal to the older couple, who would now be able to watch their grandchildren growing up instead of only seeing them occasionally. And all this was made possible with capital accumulated by Terry and Karen from their Amway business.

Amway had not been for them the instant success it had been for the Lees. It was in 1976 that Terry was introduced to a new opportunity and decided to take it up. Then he went home to tell his wife. 'She promptly went up the wall, across the ceiling and down the other side.' Karen refused point blank to go round the village with a wheelbarrow full of soap powder and pointed out that Terry could not have chosen a more appropriate day to get himself involved in such a crazy scheme—it was April 1st. Eventually they made a truce. Karen agreed that if Terry wanted to take meetings in their home she would make the coffee. It was an inauspicious beginning.

A few months passed before husband and wife were really pulling together and, though they successfully sponsored a number of people, they found progress slow. In those early days of Amway UK there were few other distributors to turn to for support and only a skeleton business structure in the country. The McCollins, however, accept most of the blame; 'We are strong characters and for a long time we simply weren't prepared to listen to our sponsor'. Then Terry, who is a surveyor, took up a job in Saudi Arabia for a year and their Amway business languished. I asked them why they did not throw in the towel. Terry laughed, 'I reckon we packed up about nine times but we just never got around to sending the kit back.' Then, more thoughtfully, he explained that they had been impressed by the tireless efforts of the Company on behalf of distributors. 'John Dodds, Stewart McArthur and others frequently came up to help with meetings. We got to know the top people personally in those days.' Above all, Terry said, he found the logic of the Amway operation inescapable; 'Once we had found the right pattern it just *had* to work'.

Then came the fateful Christmas and the remark that gave them the final push they needed. They sat down and looked at all the jobs and business ventures they had tried out. Everything but Amway seemed to have snags. Working in the Middle East, for example, was very profitable but kept Terry away from the family for long periods of time and had a bad effect on the children. So the McCollins decided to drop everything else and give Amway their full attention. Two months later they reached 21% bonus level. Three months after that they were Ruby Direct distributors. From that point on their business grew steadily. Now, with an Amway cheque for thousands of pounds arriving every month, an income which is approximately doubling itself every year, and the freedom to plan exactly how they will spend their time, life looks very good for Terry and Karen and their three children. In 1981, for example, they had five trips abroad: there was a family holiday in the Canaries; a visit to Brian and Marg Hays in America to learn more about the business; two expenses-paid expeditions to Ireland to speak at rallies and seminars; and the Amway travel seminar in Spain. Karen, understandably, values some of the less tangible aspects of their new life, such as family cohesion and the fact that Terry was able to drive their son's school football team to all their matches throughout the season. She is proud of the way they have turned their 'two-up, two-down' cottage into an attractive, substantial village house and, as she says, has already in her own mind, partly furnished the large country property of her dreams with its extensive grounds and paddocks for the children's horses. That dream would, she said, become a reality inside three years. Thereafter, the McCollins see their lives as being devoted to showing more and more people how they can be successful. Terry, fifteen years a scoutmaster, expressed his philosophy very simply, 'I love helping people who want to be helped.'

CHAPTER 11

# *Eastern Promise*

EAST ANGLIA is, in some ways, a land apart. It is on the way to nowhere, a region of wide grain fields, pink washed cottages and great wool churches, of wide flat horizons, bird sanctuaries and inlets dotted with sailing craft. This is the country which produced England's greatest landscape painters—Crome, Constable and Gainsborough. It was not hard to see why, as I travelled down lanes that made right-angled bends round fields and lingered in picturesque villages. It was a 'fresh' day. They say there is nothing between East Anglia and the Urals and there was certainly something Siberian about the wind that cut across the fields and buffetted shoppers on the narrow pavements.

I arrived by evening at Benfleet in Essex and the house of Jeff and Cath Jeffery who had kindly offered to put me up during the time that I was visiting Amway people in the area. Their welcome was warm but slightly apologetic. 'We've just got back from the West Country visiting some of our distributors,' Jeff explained. He is a cheerful, energetic man who has difficulty sitting still. He makes decisions quickly and acts on them immediately: 'I'll just go and phone Jack.' 'That door needs fixing; I'll do it now.' 'Just popping out to take these things to Joe and Susan.' Cath is the calming influence who ensures a relaxed atmosphere and anchors her husband's enthusiasm. They complement each other. It is a second marriage for both of them. And it obviously works very well.

Over supper I heard their story. People who are aware of having taken wrong turnings in life tend to be cautious and to doubt whether the future really holds for them the things they want. After fifteen years in the army Jeff knew that what he wanted above all else was freedom. He and Cath took on a chemist shop so that they could be their own bosses. They discovered that retail business brought long hours, hard work and certainly no freedom. They cut their losses and looked for something else. Jeff's friends told him that he was a natural salesman so he took a job with a large firm producing office equipment. He found that he enjoyed it and that, as he could arrange his own timetable, he had a modicum of freedom. He was also very successful. Within a few months he was top salesman for the company. He assumed that his excellent record would bring the appropriate reward and so, for a time, it did. Then things began to change, as he explained, 'It's funny how adept bosses are at changing the rules. There was me and another rep who were very successful. We were bringing in the customers and earning lots of commission. So much so that we got to the point where our salaries reached a very high level. Now, they couldn't allow that so they dropped the commission rates. That was hard because Cath and I had very little when we came together. We had to work and save hard to build our home, and we were twenty years behind most married couples. So we were on the lookout for something different, in which effort was rewarded, there was a real possibility of earning as much money as we wanted and people at the top don't change the rules when you begin to get too successful. In Amway we found it. We built to Direct distributor in nine months. We have a bigger turnover than we ever had in the shop. We have a very substantial second income and can afford some of the luxuries which didn't seem possible before—a Citroën Pallas, a new kitchen, a top quality stereo unit, more frequent holidays.'

When I came downstairs next morning Jeff announced, 'There's a café on the front at Southend where we can have breakfast. Then we can show you Leigh Village. You haven't seen it before have you? Good. Let's go then.' We drove down to the sea front and saw the sun glistening on the mud flats. We drove right onto the shingle and my host and hostess pointed out the little huts where cockles, harvested along the estuary, are boiled to create the delicacy peculiar to this corner of England. We made a leisurely exploration of the old timber houses and pubs, seemingly all mixed up with moored boats whose masts tilted at crazy angles. Then it was time to find our breakfast.

After the meal Jeff and Cath took me to my next port of call, where I was to meet a lady I shall never forget.

### *A reason for going on*

In 1978 Jenny Vanderson was heart-broken, worn down by financial worry, and concerned for her two small children. There were difficulties in her marriage. She and her husband were still sharing a house they could not sell. He was unemployed. She was fitting in three part-time jobs around caring for her little boy and girl and their home. Life was nothing but a joyless, uphill struggle against what must have appeared insuperable odds. She was certainly not in the frame of mind to respond positively when another mum waiting with her at the school gates offered to show her a business idea. She had no time, no money, no energy and no interest. She had no interest because she, herself, came from a business background. Her parents manufactured lampshades and Jenny knew all about the problems of the self-employed—increasing amounts of capital tied up, customers who did not pay their bills, cash-flow difficulties, long hours, stress.

But Rita Tribe—the other mum—persisted. She showed Jenny the Amway opportunity and Jenny grabbed it, even though she had to borrow the nine pounds it took to get started. She had no car. She had no self-confidence. She had no babysitters. Her only free evening was Saturday but she gladly devoted it to Amway because, as she told me, 'I didn't want to go on for evermore working the hours I was working for a pittance'. Rita worked the business with her (and continued till Jenny went Direct). Success was not dramatic—or would not have seemed so to many people—but to Jenny her progress was remarkable. Within weeks she could stop worrying about paying the gas bill. Within nine months her £22 a week pittance had been replaced by an income of around £70 a week. Within a year she had reached Direct distributor level and bought her first car—a £300 'banger'.

Jenny now looks back on those first few months with affection. 'Amway gave me a reason for going on and helped to take away the pain which anyone who experiences a divorce must feel. I had two choices: I could have let the divorce sweep me away and destroy me or I could build a fantastic business to give my children security and prove to other people that you can do anything if you want to. Before I went out to meetings I used to listen to an Amway tape so that I could adjust my frame of mind and go out as a positive distributor able to help others and not someone who took her own problems with her.' I knew what Jenny meant. I recalled someone else on my tour telling me that 'action conquers fear'. Sitting before me was a brave lady who was living proof of that dictum. She told me how she had overcome her initial reluctance over retailing by telling herself, 'If I sell two products we shall eat tonight'.

Jenny's is an incredible story of triumph over both external difficulties and internal tensions. She told me how she had grown in self-confidence. She was convinced that what she had done anyone could do. 'Amway brings out that person that's been longing to come out for years. Amway has the magic of making you appear more confident and therefore you become more confident.'

She laughs now at some of the experiences which must have been quite painful at the time. 'I used to have an old three-piece suite with torn chintz covers. Before a meeting I used to sew up the holes and then get my personally sponsored distributors to sit on the worst patches to cover them up. I can't put into words the feeling I had when I walked into a shop and bought a thousand pound Italian three-piece suite. It's so exciting when you see your dreams come true. I had forgotten how to dream. Life had been too hard. So I had to sit down with the children and relearn. And those kids have been marvellous, they have driven me on from goal to goal. Some people make children an excuse for not building an Amway business. In fact children ought to be the biggest reason for going to the top.'

Going to the top Jenny certainly is. She has risen through the levels since 1978 to the point where Diamond is only just around the corner. As well as financial stability and a secure future she has found happiness with someone else and will soon be settling into a second marriage.

As our conversation drew to a close, she smiled and said 'I'm going to share with you my biggest and most private dream of all. We will soon have all the money we need. After that I plan to buy a thatched cottage with a piece of land attached big enough to build an orphanage for twenty children. I have an architect building me a model. When I have that, it will motivate me so much that I'll get to Crown level really fast. After all, to achieve my dreams all I've got to do is help other people to build theirs.'

*'Fred said it wouldn't work'*

During its first nine years in Britain the organisation has brought to the fore a number of striking personalities; men and women who have become well known and much in demand as energetic leaders, entertaining speakers, people who inspire great respect and affection. I was about to meet one of them.

Pete and Vera Hedges have one of the fastest growth rates in Amway. They started their business in February 1980 and within a year had built it to the Pearl level. Within eighteen months they were earning a very substantial second income and Pete gave up his job. An Emerald distributorship soon followed and with it the usual perks—new furniture, house, car, etc. This success meant, of course, that they had also built a large, thriving group—a group of close-knit people who loved them and followed their lead. Striking proof of this came two years after the start of their business. From the beginning they had had a personal dream, of filling the local cinema with their Amway friends and they achieved that in style when they held a rally in the picture house at Basildon, packing the building to capacity with 750 people and having, on the stage, 19 Direct distributor couples.

The really interesting thing about this story, however, is not the extraordinary achievement but the husband and wife team behind it. Pete and Vera do not come from the 'executive bracket'. They were not educated or trained to leadership. They were unskilled workers in a large cigarette factory. Five days a week they slogged amidst the machines and the noise, getting up at 5 am to go to work, often putting in overtime to earn a bit extra. Evening and weekend relaxation largely revolved round the 'telly'. They were in a rut, like millions of other couples in this country, vaguely dissatisfied with their lot but unable to do anything about it. Pete had worked out a way to retire at 60, thus 'beating the system' by five years but that was the limit of his ambition. They were a cheerful couple but basically kept themselves to themselves. They were not obvious 'organisers' and, as for public speaking, they would have died rather than stand up in front of other people. Now they are one of the most popular Amway couples nationwide. Requests to address rallies pour in from all over the country. When they spoke at National Convention 1982 they had 10,000 people in hysterics and were greeted with a rapturous standing ovation.

In a few short months, fame and fortune have come to this quiet Essex couple, basically because Amway has brought out talents they did not know they possessed. It is partly the voice. Pete is a chirpy Cockney and has the quick wit popularly associated with that breed. Those of an older generation who can remember Max Miller and Tommy Trinder would readily see in Pete a similarity to those great music hall comics.

When I met him at his Basildon home, he told me how it had all started. Vera had been asked by someone at work to go to a 'business meeting'. With great difficulty she had prevailed on Pete to go with her. Neither had been very impressed with the Amway plan but Pete went back to see the distributor again and, to Vera's surprise and annoyance, he came home with a starter kit. It took them a couple of weeks, he said, to see the real potential, in the business, 'but when we did, we ran with it'.

He bustled about making tea and finding biscuits and talking as he did so.

'It's really Fred I 'ave to thank for our success in Amway,' he said pushing a loaded tray through the serving hatch. To my obvious question, 'Who's Fred?' he replied 'Well Fred was one of the blokes who told me it wouldn't work. We went round the factory trying to interest people in the business. Some joined. But others gave us a lot of stick. They used to call me "Soapy Joe" and other names. Then one day this fellow called Fred really got my goat. He said "You surprise me Pete. You and Vera are both earning good money, yet here you are scrabbling around for pennies by selling soap." That annoyed me. You see Fred wasn't willing to try Amway but he was determined that no-one else should succeed in it either. So I made up my mind to show 'im. When we went Direct and our first big monthly cheque came through—over £1,200—I 'ad it photostated four 'undred times. An' I left copies of it all over the factory. I even stuck one on me 'ead. An' I went up to Fred and I said, "You know that business you used to laugh at? Well bloomin-well laugh at this." But, lookin' back, I'm really grateful to Fred and the others, because I realise they gave us the determination to make Amway work.'

We settled in comfortable armchairs and Pete took an appreciative swig of tea. 'Another advantage we had,' he said, 'was absolutely no business experience. All we knew about Amway was what our uplines had shown us. So we copied it. We didn't try to be clever and invent new methods—and that's a mistake some people make—we just did what successful people did. That was simple and logical—an' it worked.'

'You're obviously an extrovert character, Pete,' I commented. 'That must have helped in building the business.'

He shook his head earnestly. 'But I wasn't, you see, not before Amway I wasn't. Now I feel I can do anything. I don't care what I do. Again, I have to thank those who told me it wouldn't work. You see, some people said Amway was a racket and that I was conning people. Now, I've never conned anyone in my life. I genuinely believed I was helping people by giving them the Amway opportunity. It made me angry that people thought me dishonest and I was determined to show 'em.'

Many distributors had told me that Amway had changed their personalities but no-one had given me such dramatic proof. In Pete Hedges I could begin to see how and why such a transformation could take place: Suppose that everyman has a 'closed box' inside him full of all sorts of creative talents and qualities. The box remains shut because he does not need or does not choose to use its contents. His ordinary life makes no extraordinary demands upon him. He does not even realise he possesses that hidden potential. Then something fresh confronts him, something which seems to contain exciting new possibilities. And *that* is the key which unlocks the box. The moment he says '*I* can do that' is the moment he throws back the lid and finds the resources he needs for the challenge he now sets himself.

The exciting possibility Pete Hedges saw in Amway was the possibility of being able to pack up his job, to 'beat the system' still more decisively. It was a great day for him when he walked through the factory gates for the last time, having lopped eighteen years off his 'sentence'.

Pete refilled my cup. 'One thing I must tell you,' he said, with an uncharacteristically serious expression on his face, 'is that I couldn't have done any of it without Vera. She drives me on. I might be the front man, standing up on stage making witty speeches but she's behind me all the time. It's a team effort.' He sat back in his chair. 'Well it's all team work, innit? It's because of our team, our group, that we're going to the top. When we go Diamond it's like climbin' a mountain and plantin' the flag. We'll do it mainly to encourage the group, so that they'll follow our lead and reach the mountaintop, too.'

*A family business*

What Pete said about his group, which numbered 3–4,000 distributors, held true, I felt, for all the Essex leaders I met. They are all very close. They hold frequent rallies and seem to be a great support to each other. For example, Ruby Directs Mick and Debbie Brooks enthused about the help they were given when Debbie was in hospital. She had been in the business only a few weeks (it was not until later that Mick became convinced about Amway and started to help her) but her colleagues looked after her young son and her home, visited her and filled the house with flowers for her return. Their Amway story was one of having been rescued from near financial ruin and emotional breakdown (they had to fight a costly legal battle with the local council who wanted them to pull their house down) and attained financial security, holidays in America and a Mercedes coupé. No wonder their ten-year-old son says he wants a starter kit for his eighteenth birthday.

Children provide a motivation for many Amway people to build their businesses. Pete Hedges was very proud of the fact that both of his married daughters were successful distributors. Pip and Ros Hornby told me of the couple in their group who have a little girl suffering from spina bifida and who see Amway as a means of providing the best equipment and treatment for her. The Hornbys are Pearl distributors, and giving their four children a good start in life was certainly a reason for them to build the business. Now that Pip has given up the 'rat race' of insurance underwriting and the other part-time jobs he used to do to make ends meet he certainly sees more of the youngsters.

'Family': so much of what I had seen in Essex seemed summed up in that word. I had met conventional families, single parent families, second marriages and seen what difference Amway was making to people in varied domestic circumstances. And I had seen how all of them felt themselves to be part of another, much bigger family.

CHAPTER 12

# *Commuterland*

DR JOHNSON said 'When a man is tired of London, he is tired of life'. But the London he loved was not the sprawling urban mass we know today. He could walk from one end of the city to the other in less than an hour. What would he have to say, I wonder, about the world's fourth largest metropolitan area, with all its busyness, glamour and squalor. Would he still be proud of the genius, skills and industry which maintain London as the financial and artistic centre of the world or would he agree with that later poet who wrote,

> London town's a fine town
> And London sights are rare
> London ale is bright ale
> And brisk's the London air
> But busily goes the world there
> And drowsily blinks the eye
> And London town of all towns
> I'm glad to hurry by?

I know people who would never live anywhere else but I confess my own sympathies lie with Masefield. Yet to London and the South-east I had ultimately come on the last stage of my tour. Would I learn any more here in this area which absorbs a quarter of the nation's population and a third of its wealth?

### *'I loved my job, but . . .'*

In the days before the horseless carriage, Hatfield was a leisurely day's ride from London. Courtiers, ministers and men of affairs coming down the Great North Road stopped here for the night before completing their journey to the capital. The Tudors appropriated the rambling, red-bricked palace built here by the bishops of Ely. It was in the garden of that palace that Elizabeth I sat, reading beneath an oak tree, when the news was brought to her that she was Queen of England. Elizabeth's successor, James I, gave the estate to his first minister, Robert Cecil, and Cecil built a magnificent new house on the site. The Cecils, marquesses of Salisbury, live to this day in that Jacobean mansion, overlooking acres of parkland. Hatfield House combines the features of an impressive monument and a lived-in home. It is a place I love to visit when I have the time. On a fine, early spring day I made the time.

Dutifully following the guide as she pointed out the features of the Marble Hall, the Grand Staircase and the various state rooms, I found myself studying the other tourists who had, like me, paid their 80 pences for the privilege of looking round this historic building. An elderly American couple asked a succession of questions about Mary, Queen of Scots (who had been dead a quarter of a century before Hatfield House was built). A young couple were so pre-occupied with their two-year-old's desire to pull, chew or jump on the ancient treasures, that they probably missed the guide's description. A group of OAPs pointed out to each other the porcelain, the silver, the clocks and commented how difficult it must be to keep everything dusted. An earnest young man asked erudite questions about the family portraits and pointed out to his girl friend the pictures which were 'obvious' copies.

Why do the 'stately homes of England' hold such an undying fascination for natives and visitors alike? They represent an era few of us would like to go back to, when a wealthy minority lived off the labour of an oppressed peasantry. In France that disparity finally erupted in bloody revolution. Here, political and economic change were slower but no less inexorable. So why, in our democratic age, do we travel in our coachloads to these monuments of bygone social distinction?

Much of the answer lies in the sheer breadth of life these ancient mansions represent. In these enormous buildings imagination could be allowed free rein. Wealth and power could command on a lavish scale. The finest craftsmen could be hired – masons, carpenters, plasterers, painters and carvers. Agents scoured the continent to bring back great works of art. Gardens were laid out in the grand manner, regardless of cost; river courses were changed, villages moved, lakes and hills created, just to provide pleasing vistas for fine lords and ladies. However much we may disapprove of privilege, there is in all of us a longing to have things 'just right'. Most housewives hanker after a beautiful and labour-saving kitchen. Many of us have visions of our ideal garden. The collector longs for the rare specimen which will complete his set. 'Completeness' is, indeed, an elusive quarry and in a place like Hatfield House you feel that it was made captive and enjoyed. Certainly completeness of life is a dream that inspires people to join Amway and persevere in it to acquire those things which they lack.

Norman and Maggie Barnes, who live within a couple of miles of Cecil's great house, are among those looking for the complete life. Norman came over from Canada ten years ago. He was a dedicated radiographer and was attracted by the scope of our National Health Service. It was while working that he met Maggie who was also a radiographer. Meeting people and being able to help care for their health was something they both found fulfilling – up to a point. Yet the job had its frustrations. Maggie loved the work but found herself so heavily pressed in a busy hospital that, as she said, 'I found myself referring to people as just an arm, a leg or a skull. The human aspect had gone.' For his part, Norman found restricted finance and red tape in the Health Service did not allow him to be progressive. He grew frustrated and left radiography to join a firm of medical suppliers. By this time the couple were looking for a business of their own; one that would be fulfilling and in which reward would be proportionate to effort. They thought of buying a free house or running a general store-cum-market garden.

As soon as they saw the Amway plan, Norman told me, they knew it was for them. 'The ironical thing is that I had seen the plan once before and turned it down. It was back in Canada in 1966. I was a clinical tutor in radiography and one of my students introduced me to Jim Jantz, from Alberta, who showed me the plan. I said I wasn't interested. I loved my work. I had my career in front of me. I was young and money seemed to be no problem. I often wonder what would have happened if I'd answered differently and followed Jim Jantz's example—he's a Crown Ambassador now. On the other hand,' Norman added philosophically, there's a right time for everything'.

Second time round, in 1981, Norman did not make the same mistake. He and Maggie worked their new business enthusiastically and successfully. 'All our friends were getting into Amway as soon as they saw the plan,' said Maggie. 'We were just so enthusiastic that everyone wanted to do it.' They reached the Direct distributor level inside a year. By then Maggie had given up her job. They have planned their progress carefully. With five strong legs already they can confidently look forward to reaching the Diamond level. That will enable them to have the 'complete' life they dream of. It includes: two homes (one in U.K. and one in Canada), a canal boat, marlin-fishing expeditions to the South Pacific, and horses for the children – That and a life based upon the principles of meeting and helping lots of people. The dream that the Barnes are putting together is one of an unrestricted lifestyle, not limited by shortage of time or money. That was something that the Cecils of Hatfield certainly enjoyed.

### *'The neighbours thought we were crooks'*

There could hardly be a greater contrast than that between the splendid, spacious Hatfield House and the crowded terraces of South Norwood. I had come right across London and threaded my way through miles of swarming city streets to reach this part of SE25, an area whose people still vividly remember the apalling race riots of 1981. Only one significant difference marked the house where John and Gillian Appleyard lived—there was a gleaming Daimler Sovereign parked outside. A tall, thin young man welcomed me with a vice-like handshake and ushered me in.

I do not know what I was expecting but the interior of that house certainly came as a shock—bare boards, walls of unadorned plaster, woodwork innocent of paint. 'It's a shambles, isn't it?' John commented cheerfully and I did not contradict him. 'It's a homesteading house.' He explained that the local council made a point of buying up empty houses and selling them cheaply to couples who, with the aid of loans, would renovate them and improve their value. He and Gillian had bought this house because it was all they could afford, thinking that it required little more than redecorating. When they examined it closely they found that the plumbing was decrepit, the wiring dangerous and most of the woodwork had dry rot. The house had to be gutted. 'It's a palace now, compared to what it was,' he assured me. We stood in the half-finished kitchen while John made coffee. 'People told us that we'd never build an Amway business in an area like this,' he said, 'but we've proved them wrong. Working class people round here take some convincing but once they're committed, they're really committed. Most of them have nothing to lose.'

When we were sitting in the one room that the Appleyards have so far made reasonably comfortable, and we had been joined by Gillian, they told me their story. John left school at fifteen. Eighteen years and fourteen jobs later he had got almost nowhere. He had set himself up as a small-time builder. The hours were long, the rewards meagre and the difficulties great. By virtue of the fact that Gillian was working too they managed to buy a house which no-one else wanted for six years and every spare penny went into its renovation. In the early days they 'camped' in one room, cooked on a camping stove and had to use a neighbour's bath and lavatory. Life was a slog and it never really occurred to them that it might be anything else.

They were shown the Amway opportunity by someone they met by chance, whom they had not seen for years. 'And did that make all the difference?' I asked. 'Not a bit of it,' John replied. 'We made a disastrous start. Gillian sold a neighbour some products and she didn't like them. My best friend told me Amway was a load of rubbish. The result was we did nothing for eight months. Our sponsor phoned once or twice a month to see how we were getting on. Gillian usually answered the phone and made excuses. "John's not in", "We're too busy", "We don't know anyone". I was getting fed up with the hassle. Then, one Friday, I went to collect my pay from the firm I was doing contract work for and the bloke said, "Sorry, John, they've gone bust. There's no money." That shattered me. It was a six-month contract down the drain. I'd put everything into it and now I was out of a job. We were up to our eyes in work and debt on the house.' Gillian was even more distressed. She had seen it all before: her father had had his own building business and she knew only too well the problems of the self-employed. 'Then to cap it all,' John continued, 'our sponsor phoned that evening. I took the phone and told him we had enough on our plate without Amway. We weren't going to do it. His reply was "Look John, just come along to a business meeting tomorrow night – just for my sake". I weakened a bit and agreed but when we set off to the meeting I put our starter kit in the boot so that we could give it back.'

'What changed your mind?' I asked. 'There was a man called Gordon Wadey speaking. He gave us pencils and paper and asked us to compare what we wanted out of life with what we had now—income, house, car, hours of work, money in the bank. He made me angry—not with him; with myself, with the system, with England, the government. I realised I'd reached my middle thirties, the age when a man should have made some impact on life. Instead I was working all the hours God sends—for what? Gillian and I went out and sat in the car and I said "That bloke's right". And Gillian said "What are we going to do about it?" And we both agreed to commit ourselves to this business and damned well make it work.'

Make it work they did. No difficulties stood in their way. Gillian remembered the first time they held a business meeting. 'It was after hours in a hairdressing salon. John propped his board up in a basin and nearly had to bend double to write on it. My hands were trembling almost uncontrollably when I demonstrated the products.' Within eighteen months they were at the Pearl level with 800 distributors in their group. They both gave up other work to devote all their energies to Amway. 'One of the greatest moments of my life,' John said, 'was when we had a rally for our group and in front of everyone I took a hammer and smashed my alarm clock. We're not rich—yet,' he added. 'We've more than replaced our previous incomes and we've bought a super car. But above all we've got freedom and I wouldn't trade that for anything.' Gillian suddenly burst out laughing. 'The neighbours thought we were crooks for a while. They knew John had given up building and suddenly this Daimler appeared outside. It made them terribly curious.' She told me some of her plans for the future—to get the house improvements finished and move; to start a family, secure in the knowledge that they can provide for their children; to buy a really lovely bungalow for her parents.

We chatted long over a snack lunch. Much of their excited talk was of their distributors—such as the successful lawyer who is deliberately cutting down his professional commitments to devote more time to Amway and who started a Polish relief fund to send L.O.C., clothes and other items to that afflicted country. 'We have a collection for Poland at all our training meetings now,' he added. After lunch some distributors walked in to ask advice from their uplines. I took my leave. John and Gillian were already engrossed in someone else's problems as I picked my way across builders' debris to the front door.

*Never too young to learn*

I threaded my way through suburban streets to a cul-de-sac of semi-detached houses in Merton. A pretty young woman opened the door, offered me coffee and apologised that her fiancé was late. Mike Atkins and Lynn Rathband were probably the youngest Amway distributors when they signed up in September 1980 (he was twenty and she, eighteen). Having since then reached the Ruby level, they have proved that lack of years is no drawback if you have determination. For them Amway has meant being able to start married life in a house they could otherwise not have afforded, Mike being able to give up a job he did not really enjoy, and being able to plan to start their family sooner rather than later.

They sat side-by-side on the sofa—Lynn, attractive and sensible (like the good personal secretary she is from 9.0 to 5.0) and Mike, slim, moustached and pensive—and explained the problems they had faced as an engaged couple. 'It was hard on our parents,' Lynn said, 'having the phone ringing all the time and people calling to talk or collect products. They have been very good about it but it has been a strain at times; Mike's room is jammed full of Amway boxes and when we want to see people here we have to negotiate about which room we can use. I think they were also worried in case we'd got into something that was no good. They took a lot of convincing but I showed them our first 21% cheque when it came and they haven't said anything against Amway since.'

I asked them if they found it difficult to sponsor older people. 'Strangely enough,' said Mike, 'that's easier than sponsoring people of our own age. Most of our friends live flitty kinds of lives, changing their boy friends and girl friends, going to discos and parties, all the time. They find it odd that we prefer to spend our time building a business. The accepted theory is that you spend two or three years having a good time, then settle to the hard reality of life. I tell them that we are going to spend two or three years establishing our business. When we've done that we'll be able to buy our own disco if we want.' 'So,' I suggested, 'you have missed out on your social life because of Amway?' Lynn shook her head. 'Not at all. We've made so many new friends and they're all really nice people. We didn't really know what friendship meant before we came into this business.' Mike nodded his agreement. 'You soon learn who your real friends are. There was one couple we used to be very close to. We showed them the Amway opportunity and they turned it down. But they didn't just do that; they took every chance to knock it and put others off joining. It's so sad, because they really need this business; they want to start a family and they can't afford to and his job is not very secure.' He shrugged. 'People are odd.'

I looked at this likeable couple with old heads on young shoulders and wondered if they realised how mature their attitude was. It was almost as if they had read my thoughts. 'We had to make older people take us seriously,' Mike said. 'So we deliberately dressed smartly. We learned quickly all we could about the business so that, instead of just dismissing us as kids who knew nothing about life, they had to admit that we really were experienced about Amway, if nothing else. My ex-boss is a case in point.' He explained that when he had handed in his notice his employer had asked him what he was going to do. I told him I'd got my own business and that I expected to be earning £25,000 p.a. by the end of the year. He laughed. When I offered to show him the business he turned me down. A couple of months later I heard that, due to company changes, his job had suddenly become very insecure. I phoned him and said "Look, I've got some business I want to discuss with you. What are you doing next Wednesday at 8.0?" He said, "Nothing". So we went and showed him and his wife the business and they joined.'

Lynn smiled. 'That happens so much now. Friends who used to laugh at us are thinking of getting married. They're looking for rented flats or trying to get mortgages. But we are moving into our own house. They're beginning to realise they could have been in the same position. It's sad, really.'

As I drove away I was still thinking of the last thing Mike had said. I asked him about the future and he had replied. 'What we really want to do is have some say in the running of this business. That means we have to be at least at Diamond level.' He looked at me earnestly. 'You realise Amway is going to change this country,' he said. 'Well we want to be helping to make the important decisions that are going to be so influential.' I knew, as the repetitive streets and houses passed by, that I had been listening to the future of Amway. If there were many more Mikes and Lynns around that future was in good hands.

*'Success is not sinful'*

> '. . . With a pair of opera glasses
> You could see to Hackney Marshes
> If it wasn't for the houses in between'

The plaintive refrain of the old music hall song ran through my mind as I travelled the brick-lined miles of inner suburbia but gradually the city loosened its grip and I emerged into leafy Surrey. In a lovely detached house overlooking National Trust land at the end of a private road I found Gordon and Ruth Wadey, Diamond Direct distributors. The Wadeys live a life that most couples in their thirties would envy. Parked in the driveway is a gleaming, expensive car. (Cars are Gordon's passion and when we met he was trying to decide whether his second vehicle should be another Mercedes or a Porsche.) There is an *au pair* to help with the two small children. They both play golf two or three times a week. Being full-time in Amway involves, on average, four evenings a week, though they do in addition devote several hours to organising meetings and helping individual distributors. Their five Amway years have brought other perks such as jewellery, a mink coat and travel. They have come a long way. The girl who always wore hand-me-down clothes and the young man who bought and sold cars to augment his salary have been left far behind.

Ruth was the daughter of missionary parents in Australia. When she grew up she, too, went into full-time Christian work. When she met Gordon she was employed by Trans-World Radio, a Christian broadcasting service which she had set up in London. At the time he was a computer engineer with IBM. Gordon enjoyed the work but hated having to commute into the city every day. Deep down he wanted to be his own boss. Soon after their marriage they made plans to emigrate to Australia where

Ruth's family lived and where they believed it would be easier to set up in business for themselves. It was while they were visiting relatives in Australia and looking into the possibilities of settling down there that they came across Amway products. Ruth was impressed and, on their return, she joined in the UK purely in order to obtain the goods at wholesale rates.

For months that was all there was to it. They moved to their present house using their joint salaries to raise the necessary mortgage. Then Ruth became pregnant and their income took a tumble. It was about that time that they learned how an Amway business really operates. Gordon suddenly became excited by the possibilities of high income and independence. Until then he had left Amway entirely to Ruth. Now he came in, absolutely determined to build a business quickly. Within five months the Wadeys were earning £1,000 a month and they were Ruby Direct distributors. Ruth recalled how the Amway 'bomb' burst.

'Gordon phoned our sponsors, Ken and Jane Roberts, and said he needed help. Ken asked him "What do you want out of this business" and Gordon replied "Everything!". So Ken came down and the two of them sat talking far into the night. Eventually I left them to it and went to bed. At four o' clock Gordon woke me up and said "we have to sponsor fifty people this month". I replied "You must be joking. We've only just moved here. We don't know fifty people." But he was determined so we just went out and showed the plan six nights a week. My pregnancy wasn't going too well; I was pretty sick much of the time. Added to that the World Cup was on and most guys couldn't be prised away from the box. But we signed up thirty-four new distributors that month and we went twenty-one per cent.'

The momentum never stopped. The Wadeys became the most active and successful distributors in the south-east. They reached the Ruby level two months after going Direct and celebrated by fitting double glazing throughout the house (and, of course, the two men who came to fit it were sponsored into the business). They climbed steadily to Pearl, Emerald and Diamond. After two and a half active years Gordon left IBM. He admitted that he might very well have gone to the top if he had stayed with the company but, as he said 'the price of success in industry is too high. They expect you to be married to the firm and live with your wife. IBM wanted to move me all round the country, which I didn't like. Then came the occasion when I was told at two days' notice that I couldn't have the holiday I'd booked months before. That did it. I just took out of my pocket the letter of resignation that I'd written weeks before and I threw it on the boss's desk. "There you are, kiddo. I'm not coming back".'

When I asked them the secret of their dynamic success they agreed that the most important quality was sincerity. 'When you believe in something you can talk about it,' said Ruth. 'People say that when they listen to us they're convinced. That's only because we are totally convinced ourselves. As Christians we couldn't commend something to others if we didn't wholeheartedly approve of it.'

I took up the religious point quickly.

'As Christians, how do you justify this acquisition of material things?'

'Well,' said Gordon with a laugh, 'despite what some people think, success is not sinful.'

Ruth nodded and filled some detail into the argument.

'The Lord's given us minds and he intends us to use them. That's what the parable of the ten talents is all about. As you go on in Amway you really see how that works: you only get by giving. It's beautiful. As a missionary kid I knew what it meant to be poor. I was fifteen before I had my first new dress, actually bought for me in a shop. Now one of our goals is to completely support six missionary families in the field. That's the best thing that Amway will do for me.'

'Christianity and the Amway philosophy really run in parallel,' Gordon added. 'If you want to find the best positive thinking books, look in the Bible. One of the fascinating things about this business is the way Rich and Jay's ethics come right down through the lines of sponsorship. People who have lower standards either change for the better or they don't last. This business has a habit of rejecting people it doesn't like.'

'Coming back to the money thing,' Ruth went on, 'It really becomes secondary. When we received big cheques from the Company we used to get excited, photostat them and show the group. Now we just bank them quietly and get on with the real business of helping people. We get more fun paying out cheques downline and watching our groups grow. Of course, there are challenges – personality clashes and other people's difficulties to sort out – but those are the things that help you to mature. We reckon that the experience you gain reaching the Emerald level is equivalent to a degree in psychology. Certainly your sense of awareness towards life and people can only be heightened.'

### *Creatures of impulse*

Biggin Hill earned its honoured place in the history of these islands during the late summer of 1940. It was during those hot, hazy August and September days that Spitfires and Hurricanes of Fighter Command leaped into the skies from RAF Biggin Hill to counter the might of Goering's Luftwaffe. This airfield in Kent was one of the more important bases from which the Battle of Britain was won. It is still there, though partly given over now to civilian aircraft, and it filled me with nostalgia as I drove past. One of my earliest childhood memories is of watching aerial dog fights over London. They thrilled me because I was able to experience the excitement of battle while being too young to have any concept of the horror of war. That triumph of 'the Few' still strikes a patriotic spark in my breast, and I hope in the breast of every Briton.

My next port of call was a pleasant little cul-de-sac hard by the airfield. I was greeted overwhelmingly in the small hall by what appeared to be a boisterous Shetland pony but turned out to be a Pyrennean Mountain dog. It is sometimes said that owners come to resemble their pets. I could see no physical resemblance in this case but for sheer 'bounce' and enthusiasm Mandy is a superb match for her master and mistress, Alan and Sandie Niel. Like them, Mandy is a creature of impulse. Once she chased the neighbour's cat and when the moggy rushed to the haven of her own home through the specially-constructed little flap in the back door, the huge dog tried to follow, with disastrous results for the door.

Alan readily admitted that they, too, like doing crazy things. 'That's probably why we're in Amway,' he said. Sandie giggled. 'That sounds ambiguous,' she said. 'Well you know what I mean,' he replied good-humouredly. 'For instance, there was that morning last November. I woke up with a fantastic idea . . .' 'Oh, yes,' Sandie interrupted. 'I was fast asleep and he shakes me by the shoulder and says "Let's go over to Paris for our Christmas shopping." Next thing I know is we're on the ferry.'

The husband-and-wife banter between this lively couple was kept up almost non-stop throughout the few hours that I spent with them, first in their comfortable first-floor sitting room, then over a pub lunch in the local. In between, however, I did manage to squeeze their story out of them. When they were shown the Amway plan in 1980 Alan was working as an accountant and Sandie was with an in-home sales organisation. Both of them were divorcees and with an ex-wife and two children to support Alan was definitely feeling the pinch. Sandie was earning good money but she was working long hours for it and was out most evenings. There were long periods when they scarcely saw each other and that, as they said, is not a very secure foundation to build a second marriage on. The strain was beginning to show. So much so that one of Sandie's colleagues recommended that she have a look at a business which puts less pressure on people.

'We looked at the plan one Sunday,' Alan told me. 'We were quite interested and we came home to think about it. The couple who showed us gave us an L.O.C. to try out. Well, we talked about it that day but we were quite undecided. It looked good but it would mean Sandie giving up Tupperware and we didn't know whether we could afford that. We still hadn't made our minds up next morning when I went to work. When I reached the office an hour and three traffic jams later I found that Sandie had phoned a message through to my secretary. It simply said "I've sold two. How many have you sold?" Sandie chipped in 'What had happened was that two friends had come round for coffee, seen the L.O.C. on the draining board, and decided they wanted some, too.' Alan laughed 'So we really had no choice. Amway joined us; we didn't join Amway.'

But Sandie was still worried about the challenge to her other business. She was even more worried when they had their first Amway meetings at which people either did not turn up or did not join. 'It was a rally in Croydon which was the real turning point,' Alan said. 'Our sponsors took us to hear Don and Angie Nellenbach, who have Emerald businesses in the USA, Britain and Ireland. They were dynamite. They told us about all the meetings *they* had held which were flops and, yet, there they were obviously enjoying a very substantial Amway income. We came home and I said to Sandie "Look we know now that this business works. We've seen lots of people who are making it work. If we can't make it work, it's our fault, not Amway's. So we made a decision that we were going to succeed. The following week we sponsored five people.'

'We made a good start,' Sandie said. 'We made 9% in our first month.' 'No, it was 6%,' Alan corrected. I waited while they debated facts and statistics. 'Anyway,' Sandie said eventually, turning back to me brightly, 'the crunch soon came with my job. I had to go over to my distributor's house and formally resign. That meant handing in my brand new car and saying goodbye to a potential income of £15,000 a year. I cried all the way there and all the way back. I really hated Amway that day. I was still down in the dumps when Alan got home. He put his arm round me and said "Look, I'll make you a promise: when we go Direct at Christmas we'll get you a new car"—and we did.'

Six months later they were earning enough for Alan to give up his accountancy job, though he worked for a few clients at home. 'It was a bit soon,' Sandie admitted, 'but I felt sure we could build the business faster if we were both doing it all the time. The next three months weren't easy. We love being together but we had to find the right way to work together.' She lifted her voice in a cadence of shrill laughter. 'The neighbours certainly knew when we were at home. But things soon settled down. By the autumn we were earning a higher income than ever before and we haven't stopped increasing it.'

By now Sandie was sitting on the edge of her chair and the words were bubbling out, for all the world as though she were a little girl describing her first visit to the circus. 'Life is so much better,' she said. 'Alan doesn't have to dash out in the morning. His shirts don't get filthy dirty as they did when he worked in London. It's little things like that that you notice. I'd do this business for far less money. In fact, we sat down and talked about this a few months ago and we realised a funny thing had happened to us: when we joined Amway we were very money orientated because we hadn't got any. Now it's far less important. We get a kick out of watching other people change and grow in the business. We've seen people come in who are full of bitterness and gradually, as Amway gets into them they change: they get more concerned about others, more tolerant.'

I asked them if *they* had changed.

'Gosh, yes,' said Alan. 'I'll give you a funny example. One Sunday morning I suddenly said to Sandie, "You're going to think this odd but I'd rather like to go to church." And Sandie laughed and said "Strange you should say that; I've been feeling that for the last couple of weeks." We hadn't been to church in years. Now we go often. I don't know why. It just seemed the right thing to do.'

Since they were obviously in a better position than most people to judge I asked the Niels how Amway compared with other direct selling enterprises. 'It's very, very different,' Alan said. 'The back-up from the Company is spectacular—excellent delivery, sympathetic support and an ever-increasing product range. There's no competition in Amway, unlike other organisations, where agents are encouraged to vie with each other for custom. Then, again, in anything else I know of you're only as good as your next sale or your next party. When you stop your income stops. Whereas if Sandie and I were to fall ill the group would carry on and the monthly cheques would still be there. Then there's . . .'

But Sandie was bursting to interrupt.

'More than all that,' she said, 'It's the people. Amway people are special.'

### *A question of priorities*

It was mid-afternoon before I left the Niels and I decided to indulge myself by taking a circuitous route through the byeways of Kent and Sussex, through villages where greens are neatly mown and half timbered cottages sit cosily in colourful gardens. This is the land beloved by Hillaire Belloc who dreamed of

> . . . a house with deep thatch
> To shelter me from the cold,
> And there shall the Sussex songs be sung
> And the story of Sussex told.

It was thus I squandered the daylight hours and came to Eastbourne by night.

I came to the home of Paul and Liz Bartlett, who, since 1979, have done so much to pioneer the spread of Amway on the south coast.

'We never let anyone tell us they're too busy,' Paul said. 'We started in Amway with nine children and with Sundays and several evenings commited to church activities.' Paul, a soft-spoken legal executive, and his wife are keen Mormons who obviously take their religion very seriously. With a large family ranging from 4 to 18 they certainly have many commitments.

'It was really the financial pressures of bringing up a large family that made us look at Amway seriously,' Liz explained. We accumulated many debts and they weren't geting any smaller. We returned from Canada where Paul worked for a couple of years to find that inflation was running riot and money had lost its value. By the time we had bought the house—and we obviously have to have a large house—we were virtually penniless.'

Paul took up the story.

'I met a chap at our church who kept saying to me, "I've just started a part-time business." now, I was obviously supposed to say, "What business?" but I didn't rise to the bait. So one day, in desperation I suppose, he invited Liz and me round to see some of his slides. So we went and we saw the slides . . . then some more slides . . . then some more, till eventually his wife took the plunge, brought in some products and started to talk about the business. They were very new in Amway, so they really didn't make a very good job of explaining it to us but we saw enough to realise that it might be just what we needed. Of course, with my legal training, I had to look into Amway very carefully. I checked with the Department of Trade and Industry and through legal circles. What I discovered was that Amway is just about the most honest and scrupulous Company you could ever come across. Soon after that, this couple went to live in Canada, so through the Company we got in touch with Gordon and Ruth Wadey, our nearest Direct Distributors. They came down to take our first meeting for us and we filled this room with friends and neighbours. At the end of the meeting I said "Right, I'm getting in" and four other couples said, "Yes, so are we". So we got off to a really good start. We were Direct in seven months and we received our pins from Rich De Vos himself at National Convention. Now we are at Ruby level and plan to be Pearl this year.'

I spent a pleasant evening with the Bartletts. They showed me the computer they have bought for calculating bonuses and stock orders and talked happily about the Volvo estate car they have recently acquired and which is rather more comfortable than the old Austin Maxi which they had previously crammed themselves and nine children into. They talked equally happily about other people who had done better than them. 'We've never considered Amway a race,' Paul told me. 'We don't have as much time to devote to it as some others. We just saw it as a way of gaining financial stability and a comfortable way of life. That was something we certainly couldn't have otherwise. We realised when we decided to have a large family that that would entail sacrifice. Now the sacrifices are fewer.'

'And what of the future?' I asked.

'Freedom,' said Paul. 'At Diamond level I'll be able to give up my job, and then we'll have more time to devote to our church work.'

I left at last and drove down to the front. Walking along the promenade with the waves hissing on the shingle and moonlight reflected on the water I thought of the incredible variety of people I had met over the last few weeks. I had heard dramatic and exciting stories in abundance – stories of amazing wealth, of triumph over handicaps, of startling business success. But there had also been the less striking tales, the ones about people who have no desire to be high fliers, people who will never allow Amway to take the place of things they believe to be more important and yet who can use the vehicle of Amway to enrich their lives in the ways they choose to have their lives enriched. It seemed that Amway really was for anyone.

CHAPTER 13

# *Dare to Dream*

'IT WORKS.'

That was the principal opinion I had formed by the end of my tour. It was abundantly obvious to me that Amway was providing thousands of British people with not only extra income but also an extra dimension to life.

Even when looked at from a purely business point of view Amway manifestly works. The Company is a member of the Direct selling Association, and the General Manager is, in fact, a member of the council of that body. Amway is the fastest growing in-home marketing organisation in the country and will be the largest by the end of the decade.

How can we explain that success? What makes it different from any other direct selling company? At first glance, very little. Door-to-door and party-plan companies pay discounts and bonuses and combine retailing with sponsoring. Other companies manufacture excellent products, give good service and good value. When it comes down to it direct selling organisations are like cakes—they all have the same basic ingredients. What makes one taste better than another is the proportions in which those ingredients are mixed and the extra flavourings that are added.

Rich De Vos and Jay Van Andel got the basic mix just about right back in 1959 and it has been refined since. There is a precise balance of reward for effort, incentive to help others, recognition of achievement, immediate income and long term security. Over the years there have been more than two hundred attempts to copy Amway, to produce something 'like it only better'. This fact in itself is proof of Amway's success—no-one copies something that does not work. Almost every one of those two hundred or so companies has gone bust. None of them has ever come near to rivalling Amway. They changed the balance of the basic ingredients and the results were financially non-viable cakes.

But it is the added flavourings that make Amway taste special. First of all there is total integrity. When, in August 1974, financial reporter John Petty wrote a feature for the business pages of the *Daily Telegraph* he entitled his piece 'Honest Amway Comes to Britain'. He drew attention to the Corporation's rigid code of ethics and commented, 'Perhaps this unusual approach to selling compared with normal high-pressure American methods arises because the business began in a Dutch community not far from Grand Rapids, Michigan, which was noted for its moral standards.'*

When something is presented to you as whiter than white you automatically begin to look for the snag. Many people who are shown the Amway plan experience the initial reaction 'It's too good to be true'. On closer inspection, as many distributors told me, they discover that Amway really can and does deliver the goods. When Frederick Birmingham was preparing a report on Van Andel and De Vos and their organisation for the *Saturday Evening Post* he questioned Frank Cook, a successful but by no means outstanding distributor from Indianapolis. Cook had been with Amway for eighteen years. He used it as his ticket out of the rat race of advertising. Now he and his family live very well in their luxurious lakeside home. Having seen how Cook lives and runs his business, the journalist asked, almost in desperation 'Tell me, Frank, what's *wrong* with Amway'. With a laugh the other replied, 'I've been looking for years, and I give up. There's nothing wrong with Amway.'† Interestingly, the same verdict is given by most of those who quit Amway. In the States the Corporation itself conducted a survey of non-renewing distributors. They found that in every case people stopped their activities for personal reasons or lack of interest. Not one of them claimed that Amway or Amway products had in any way failed them.

Another reason for Amway's commercial success is the quality and extent of the product range. Customers and distributors alike always have new products to try out, for barely a month passes without at least one fresh item being launched. Having accustomed themselves to the quality of existing stock items, people are usually confident about experimenting with the novelties. Thus they are steadily becoming more dependent on Amway for a growing proportion of their regular and occasional purchases.

There has been a shopping revolution in the last fifteen years. Most housewives can easily remember the daily pilgrimage to the high street, the queues, the personal service. That situation was changed by the supermarket and the hypermarket. Then came the enormous growth in mail order business. The latest developments are selling through Prestel and telephone ordering. In a *Times* article dated 15 April 1982, Derek Harris wrote

* *Daily Telegraph*, 14 August 1974.
† *Saturday Evening Post*, November 1979.

> 'There are those who argue that when a family can call up mail order offers on the television set and order from their armchairs then the sector will be able to make a quantum leap forward'.

Streamlined selling techniques cut costs basically by getting the customer to do things the shop assistant used to do. We, the consumers, are becoming conditioned to this: we push our trolleys round the supermarket, fill our petrol tanks at the garage, phone or write for catalogued goods, even obtain money from little machines in the outside wall of the bank.

All this is inevitable if the product costs are to be kept to a minimum. Yet the thing most people miss about the good old days is 'personal service'; having a knowledgeable salesperson available to explain what the product will and will not do, to demonstrate and to advise. Amway is unique in that it makes available to customers a very wide range of merchandise which they can buy in their own home *and* provides the old fashioned personal service in the form of distributors who have access to all the necessary product information.

Most of Amway's distributionships are husband and wife teams and this is another great plus. No other major direct selling organisation has successfully tapped this great sort of strength. The typical party plan or door-to-door operation is regarded with disdain by most husbands as 'a little selling business for the wife'. It has a 'pin-money' image, even though some agents make good incomes. By combining the talents of both partners—and often children as well—Amway ensures that the image of the business is of something stable, secure and homely.

But the most distinctive flavouring ingredient of all is the philosophy, the *raison d'être* of Amway. At root Amway is *not* just a business, i.e. it was not conceived as a vehicle for selling products to make profit for the founders and shareholders (there are no shareholders apart from Rich and Jay). The *Saturday Evening Post* article which I have already quoted explained the purpose of Amway like this

> 'The dream of Rich De Vos and Jay Van Andel was to build a company that would offer all persons who seek it a chance to change their lives. Their dream was to offer those who work for it a chance to build their own business, set their own goals, make their own future.'

It is not easy to build an Amway business. It requires 'stickability' and constant enthusiasm. Distributors sometimes have to put up with abuse from people who insist on believing that Amway is a 'con'. What sustains most of them is the strength of their own dreams. They identify with the goal of the founders. They know what they want and they believe that with Amway they can get it. Moreover, the only route to the achievement of their goals lies through helping other people achieve theirs.

Amway Corporation welcomes fair competition but it seems unlikely that anything 'the same only better' will ever become established. The time was right for Rich and Jay when they put their idea together. Since 1959 they have built it so well that it will be very difficult for a competitor to bake a more attractive cake. Certainly, in Britain the business which started comparatively slowly has built into something very strong.

In the future, 1982 will probably be seen as a watershed in the British business. It was marked by two important events. The first was the annual convention—the biggest business meeting ever held in Britain. In years to come it will not be possible to hold a single annual gathering because no covered hall has the facilities to cope with the numbers wishing to attend. Convention '82, with its 10,000 distributors, will, therefore, be one of the highlights of Amway's history as distributors look back over the years. The other event was the opening of the impressive new Company HQ at Tongwell, which is big enough to cope with the £100,000,000 annual turnover which the Company expects to reach before the end of the decade.

*The quitters*

As with other direct selling businesses, many people join Amway for a short time and then quit. The proportion is small in comparison with Amway's major competitors. The reasons why people give up are many and varied. I spoke to quite a few (interestingly, most of them asked for their names not to be quoted). If we leave aside those who joined for a few days, then exercised their right to return their kit, the bulk of those who quit seem to do so because they find perseverence a difficult virtue to acquire. If they do not achieve quick success they become discouraged. Some whom I spoke to believed their sponsors had not helped them enough but most acknowledged that the shortcomings were their own. I encountered no bitterness, no feeling that they had been swindled. In fact most of them continue to use Amway products and remain friends with their erstwhile colleagues in the business. One couple told me that Amway had done a great deal for them in the few months they had been involved. Fortified with positive mental attitude, they had applied themselves to their other business (a guest house) with renewed vigour and enthusiasm.

*Whither Britain?*

In the first quarter of 1982 three dismal national statistics were recorded: 2,700 businesses went into liquidation (a record); unemployment stood at around 3,000,000 (a record); and British living standards fell further behind those of other leading industrial nations (OECD figures showed that out of the top twelve western nations of the EEC, Japan and the USA, Britain was in ninth position, followed only by Italy, Ireland and Greece). No manufacturing country emerged unscathed from the recession of the turn of the decade but our land certainly fared worse than most. Will there be a substantial recovery and, if so, what form will it take? We cannot answer these questions yet. What we can say for certain is that any answers will have to be new answers and they will largely emerge from below rather than being imposed from above.

In our complex and rapidly changing society governments cannot pull neat solutions out of a hat. There is no more mileage left in old dogmas: socialism, capitalism and communism are alike, ready for the museum. It will be enterprising businessmen, employees, teachers and administrators who create the new patterns of socio-economic life. They will be motivated partly—perhaps largely—by self-interest: the need to provide an alternative source of income; the desire to cushion the family against the possible loss of a job; the quest by school leavers for their own individual or co-operative business enterprises; the development of more leisure industries; the necessity of commercial diversification for financial survival; the demand for cheaper capital; and, not least of all in an age of enforced leisure, the determination to stave off boredom, gain fulfilment and do something worthwhile.

The building blocks of national prosperity will be individual initiative and achievement. As enterprising citizens experience success—and providing the framework of taxation and regulations does not stifle success—so growing demand for consumer goods and services will create wealth for the community at large. It is crystal clear to me since I completed my tour that one vehicle hundreds of thousands of British men and women will use to achieve success will be Amway. If we project the growth of existing Amway businesses into the future it is obvious that the middle 1980s will see a large number of distributors reaching the upper levels of Double Diamond, Crown and Crown Ambassador. They will be enjoying five- and six-figure incomes and the lifestyles to go with them. They will be employing secretaries and domestic help. They will be buying large houses and the furnishings to go in them. Some will be investing capital in the money markets. Others will be setting up children or relatives in their own businesses. Many will be generously supporting charities. There will be distributors whose dreams are more modest but they, too, will be making their contributions to society. Every Amway distributor who quits his job to 'go full time' in the business eases the overall employment situation. Everyone who devotes part of his increased free time to voluntary work with the young, the handicapped, the elderly or the jobless is fulfilling a useful role.

Amway stands for free enterprise—it is, I suppose, the ultimate in free enterprise. To some, of a leftish political persuasion, this may make it suspect. Yet it is difficult to see what anyone can find to object to, for the 'unacceptable face of capitalism' has no place in the Amway operation. There is no exploitation and no fostering of an economic élite. Amway represents the ultimate in equality of opportunity. Determination and industry alone ensure success in this business. Men with capital, commercial experience or influential connections cannot buy their way in at a high level. The newest recruit and the most seasoned Crown Ambassador build their businesses in precisely the same way: by 'showing the circles' to prospective new distributors. It may always be necessary for a compassionate society to care for its disadvantaged by giving financial aid—aid which comes from the taxes of the more fortunate. But Amway does offer an alternative to many disadvantaged and handicapped people. It says 'here is something you can do just as well as anyone else'. I have met blind people, single parent families, people in wheel chairs, people so poor that they had to borrow the money for a starter kit—and they have all found in Amway not only a path to financial independence but a stairway to self-esteem.

I can see no reason to doubt that Amway will be an increasingly important part of the British economic scene in coming decades. Just how important we shall have to wait and see. Yet there is one aspect of the business which is vital to Amway's success and which I would love to see taken up by people in all walks of life. It is called 'positive mental attitude' and it is basically what has made grade 'A' failures into high-flying Amway successes. One of Henry Ford's many brusque epigrams was 'Think you can, think you can't. Either way you'll be right'. One reason for this country's sluggish performance in the commercial and political arenas of the world is a lack of national self-confidence. The days of empire and Britain's moral ascendancy have departed, leaving us to a large extent unsure of ourselves and our ability to create a new international role. We are not sure whether we should be in the EEC or out of it. Our attitude towards western military defence is ambivalent. We feel ourselves powerless in the disputes of the international giants. If we are going to forge a new role for Britain in world affairs, we need to rediscover a passionate belief in our nation. We have to rekindle the conviction that we can be leaders in whatever field of expertise we choose. That change of national attitude will come as and when more *individuals* learn to believe in themselves.

*Secrets to share*

When I first projected the idea of this book there were some who said, 'Great idea, but don't you think you ought to wait a bit? By 1983 and 1984 there will be lots of fantastically wealthy people to write about.'

I am glad I did not take their advice—for two reasons. First of all I wanted to capture the picture of the early years before people's memories were blurred by success. Secondly, I did not believe that the Amway story belonged solely to the people who had achieved the Mercedes, the big houses, the financial independence and the holidays in Hawaii. The story I have tried to sketch in these pages is about people who are building their own dreams—however grand or modest those dreams may be. It is the story of thousands of people who are better off than they were before. Some are making a substantial second income. Some have been able to give up dull, routine jobs. Some are building security for the future. Some are providing for their children's education or, simply, taking away the worry about the weekly bills.

In a way, what is more important than the actual financial, return is the fact that Amway people are enjoying what they are doing. Unlike successful participants in other enterprises, they are not reaching their objectives by hacking their way through a highly competitive jungle. When Roger and Babs Powdrill reached the Diamond level there was an *Amagram* feature on them in which they were quoted as giving this advice to anyone who wanted to follow in their footsteps:

> 'Get to know people closely and make sure that they are fully aware that you believe in their ability to succeed and develop along with yourself, into mature, caring and, above all, successful people.'

With an attitude like that it is not surprising that so many of the distributors I met were relaxed, cheerful folk who seemed to have plenty of time for others; people who had rediscovered the value of marriage; people who were enjoying family life in a new way.

Above all, the Amway story is the story of men and women

who have discovered something to believe in and strive for. They know the business works and that if they make it work for them they can have whatever they want in this world. They have a new hope which has lifted them out of their old rut and given them an altogether wider field of vision. I remember what Mary Castell said: 'When most people get to fifty they give up. We've just reached our half century and we know that the second is going to be more exciting than the first.'

'Exciting'—I would like a pound for every time I heard that word during my Amway tour. Yet, perhaps, for the readers of this book the *most* exciting fact is that the Dream Makers' secrets are not really secrets at all, because they are willing to share them with anyone.